G. W. HURLEY
"BOOKSHOP"
27-29 HIGH STREET
BURNHAM-ON-SEA
SOMERSET
TEL: 782554
VAT No. 131 3659 87

Sportsviewers Guide
RUGBY LEAGUE

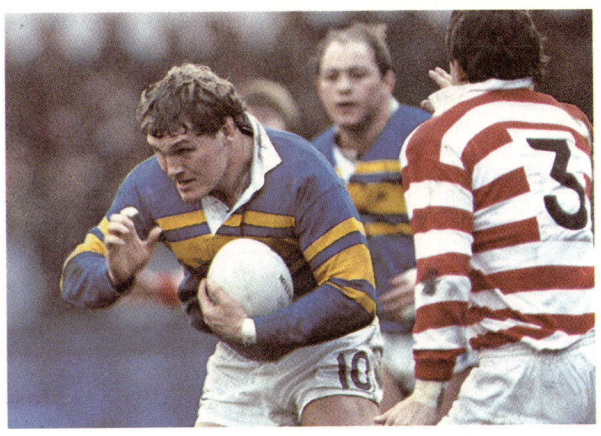

John Clemison

DAVID & CHARLES
Newton Abbot   London

Contents

Watching rugby league   4–7
What to look for in televised matches.

History and development   8–13
How the game was created by a northern splinter group from rugby union and in the 1980s has found new footholds in Wales, London and Kent.

Rules and terminology   14–21
An explanation of the laws with special sections on the iron rule of referees like Fred Lindop and on the 'sin bin'.

Stars   22–31
Profiles of the leading characters on and off the field — players, administrators and club chairmen.

Road to the top   32–37
Why rugby league has to 'poach' from rugby union and how changes in the education system have helped the professional game.

Cups and competitions   38–47
The league's bold move to stage the Challenge Cup final at Wembley has paid off and it is the showpiece among the game's four main competitions — ahead of the championship, the premiership and the John Player Cup. This section also looks at the role of sponsorship.

Equipment   48–53
A run-down on the players' kit, from padding to studs. How tough are rugby league players?

Venues   54–59
How old-fashioned grounds are being improved with the aid of a central fund and how sharing with soccer clubs helps to raise standards.

People in the media   60–61
The spirit of Eddie Waring lives on even after his retirement with his catchphrases such as 'early bath' and 'up-and-under' although his successors are trying to foster a greater understanding of the game.

Statistics   62–64
All-time individual and club records are listed together with the winners of the main events in recent seasons.

British Library Cataloguing in Publication Data
Clemison, John
   Rugby league — (Sportsviewers guides)
   1. Rugby league — History
   I. Title   II. Series
   796.33′3′09   GV944.85

ISBN 0–7153–8504–6

The Sportsviewers' Guide to Rugby league was produced and designed by
Siron Publishing Limited of
20 Queen Anne Street, London W1,
Series editor: Nicholas Keith
Photographs by Tommy Hindley and Tony Henshaw of Professional Sport.

© David & Charles (Publishers) Ltd 1983.
All rights reserved. No part of this publication may be reproduced, stored in a retrieval system or transmitted in any form or by any means, electronic, mechanical, photocopying, recording or otherwise, without prior permission of David & Charles (Publishers) Limited.

Typeset by ABM Typographics Ltd, Hull
and printed by
Printer Industria Gráfica SA
Cuatro Caminos, Apartado 8,
Sant Vicenç dels Horts,
Barcelona, Spain DLB 17344-1983
for David & Charles (Publishers) Limited
Brunel House   Newton Abbot   Devon

Foreword

The expansion of rugby league beyond its traditional northern boundaries to Fulham, Maidstone, Cardiff and Carlisle, has created a big new audience for the game. This book fills two major needs. It gives a comprehensive and lively guide to new devotees, while at the same time giving additional background to the game for existing enthusiasts and supporters.

All aspects of the rugby league game are covered: its formation, history and development; its essential features and the special qualities and laws that set it apart from rugby union; the game's rapid growth among amateur clubs and schools; its great personalities, on and off the field, and a particularly fascinating section on television and other media coverage.

The comments on television's coverage of the 13-a-side game were obviously of particular interest to me. TV coverage has expanded in the past few years with the arrival of ITV's *RL Action* in northern viewing areas on Mondays complementing the BBC Saturday coverage of top matches. There are some salty and critical observations on the coverage and some telling points are made.

Here is a book full of interest, information and lively comment, an informative and entertaining guide to a game rapidly increasing in popular appeal. It should be on the bookshelf of every player, administrator, observer, reporter and fan, old or new, of a magnificent and full-blooded game.

Keith Macklin

Watching rugby league

Television can never give a true picture of any sport because, in essence, it is a tunnel view of the world. Cameras are trained, by and large, to follow the ball and, as anyone who watches live sport regularly will testify, it is often what happens away from the ball that determines the result of a match.

In rugby league, the cameras show only the immediate action — the crunching tackle on the ball-carrier or the ball as it sails between the posts. It is by no means a deliberate distortion of the game: it is the nature of a medium which to be digestible to the viewer must inevitably present only a limited amount of information. The trouble is that most viewers accept this as reality.

To enjoy rugby league on television, you need to know what to look for. If the cameras do not give that wide a view, you will have to imagine it, just as you have to build up a composite picture in your mind of the field-placings at a cricket match.

To win a rugby league match, a team has to score points, and the quickest way of amassing them is by touching down tries. Yet in front of the players are another thirteen whose aim it is to stop them doing so. In order to break down that barrier, the rugby league player must search for or create gaps in the other side's defences.

He does so by a number of methods: by forcing the other team to commit too many players to tackling, thereby creating spaces on the wings; by switching play from one touch-line to the other to pull the opposition away from the traditional man-to-man marking; by tiring the opposition so that it can no longer keep up with the attacking team's pace; by drawing two tacklers and then slipping the ball away to an unmarked member of his team; or simply by kicking (usually along the ground) to gain a scrum farther upfield, which the attacking team hopes will provide possession.

There are other ways of scoring, of course, but the most successful league teams are the ones that can play at full pace for eighty minutes, absorb as many tackles as the opposition can throw at them, jink their way past the cover, and with the intelligence to vary their play sufficiently to outwit the marshalled defence.

There is more to rugby league than running with the ball or kicking at goal. Whereas in many other sports, several members of the team may be able to rest for a while, every player in a league team is involved for the whole eighty minutes of a match simply by being there. While football goalkeepers complain about not having enough to do on cold days, the rugby league player, whatever his position, has to concentrate on presenting his opponents with as many problems as he can, both in attack and defence.

Only when a player is kicking at goal (the defending team is not allowed to charge at the kicker in league) can players earn a moment's breather. Not even when a player is injured (unless his presence on the ground might interfere with play) does the game stop, for the trainer will rush on to deal with the injury while play carries on around him. It is almost a continuous game — exhausting to the player but there is never a dull moment for the spectator.

One of the pleasures of watching the game is waiting for a team that has been pressing for some considerable time to score. That is one reason edited highlights rarely give a true picture of how the game was won. A quick resumé of the tries and goals in a fifteen-minute sequence makes the game seem trivial and unsatisfying, other than to those who saw the match live. Following the sequence in which one team found the space to cut

A try — the fastest way of scoring points. This one is by O'Hara for Hull in the 1983 premiership final against Widnes.

Watching rugby league/2

through the other's defence is what watching the game is all about, no matter how dramatically the stand-off or wing plunged over his opponent's goal-line.

Watching the game live helps the viewer to appreciate coverage of rugby league on TV, but for those who cannot reach a live game, there is still plenty to be gained from following the sport from an armchair. Yet it is vital to know what to watch for. Study the patterns of the game and you will begin to understand what makes a successful rugby league side tick.

Look for the cracks in the defending team's defence; watch for the way in which teams try to tire out their opposition with barging runs in the middle of the field and by switching play from one flank to the other. Try to forget the showmanship and the humour for a moment and think of the tactics required to take a team to a touch-down or to cause the opposition to panic and so give away a penalty.

Knowing what to look for is the essence of getting the most out of viewing a game on television. This book aims to help you understand the techniques, the people and the structure of what is one of the most absorbing spectator sports ever devised.

The task of television commentators is almost impossible, but they cope with the problems commendably well. The standard technique is to name the players as they receive the ball and occasionally provide brief biographical details. To the man who is watching on the terraces at the game, however, the names hardly matter; the patterns of play are far more important.

The sight of an overlap on the outside or a gap developing in midfield is the essence of the excitement, and yet any commentary that conveyed that excitement would be well-nigh impossible to make and produce 'poor television'. One viewing technique is to switch off the commentary and watch the match in vision only. Although this means there is no 'atmosphere', the game itself takes on a totally different perspective.

Rugby league is more widespread in Britain now than it has ever been, and there will soon be only a handful of areas in the country where the game is out of reach. Already, Fulham have made their mark in London; Kent Invicta plan to bring the south-east its second professional club in 1983–4; there is talk of rugby league clubs being formed in Southend and Bristol in the near future; there is a club in south Wales (Cardiff City). The game has also spread overseas, being more successful than rugby union in Australia and on equal terms in New Zealand. France, Italy and the United States have rugby league clubs, too, although only in France has the game really developed.

The 1982–3 Australians

Many people who saw the Australian touring team demolish every home side they met on their visit to Britain in 1982–3 were given a lesson in how to play the game. The Australians were probably the hardest tacklers that British players had ever met. Their usual tactic was to devote two men to each tackle — one taking a player around the legs, the other smothering the ball in the player's arms, effectively snuffing out any chance of a pass.

In theory, it should have been possible to find a gap in the Australian defence, because putting two men into the tackle should leave the side one short elsewhere on the field. The Australians overcame that difficulty by preventing a pass to a player in support and because they were extremely fit. The moment the tackle was made, both Australian players would recover and race back to plug any gaps.

There was more to the Australian style than hard and quick tackling, however. In attack, they showed deft skills in slipping the ball out of the tackle to a supporting colleague, who always seemed to be at the tackled player's shoulder. They were quick on the break and, perhaps most important of all, they played the six-tackle rule superbly. As soon as they had been tackled five times, they sought to use the ball, either kicking for ground or by making an incisive break through the centre. That is partly because the Australians have had long experience in playing six-tackle rugby league (Britain adopted the system much later). For these reasons, they swept all before them on their visit.

The Aussie way: the 1983 Australians show how they tackle in numbers and prevent their opponent from getting the ball to a teammate.

History and development

However odious the comparisons between rugby league and rugby union, no one is allowed to forget that one grew out of the other. The league — once the Northern Rugby Football Union — was formed in the 1890s by a group of rebellious rugby union clubs in the north of England who were dissatisfied with the attitude of those who administered their game.

Anyone who has watched both codes in recent years cannot fail to see the similarities between them. However, most people do not appreciate that, after ninety years, the differences are now far more significant than the few things they have in common.

There will always be bar-room arguments about which is the more skilful, which is better to watch, which is harder to play. In the end, though, you cannot compare them. The techniques, the administration, the attitude of the players, the crowds, the television coverage, the laws, the scoring system, the history and the development of each are such that any comparison between the two sports does a disservice to both.

No one need feel ashamed for trying to compare league and union. The senior officials in each code have conducted that particular exercise in their minds time and again. Even today, ninety years after the formation of the league, directors of important league clubs try to 'win one over' on the union — comparing crowd sizes, pointing out the slightest lapse into professionalism by a leading union player, arguing that the union ought to 'come clean' about expenses payments. They do not help the cause of rugby league, either.

Rugby league is a sport in its own right and can safely be looked at in isolation. It can be richly entertaining or incredibly dull. It has its triumphs and its disasters. Though its laws are simpler than those ruling many other sports, one or two of them are bewilderingly complicated — so much so that the top-flight referee is as much a politician as a party chairman. As with any other sport, the more you know about the game, the more you will appreciate watching it.

Why is rugby league so often compared with rugby union? Because that is where it all started. Rugby union began its rise to a national sport a century ago as a game that was learnt in the public schools and which was predominantly a middle-class sport (as indeed was soccer at that time). Rugby union clubs sprang up most noticeably in the well-heeled suburbs as a character-building, Saturday afternoon activity for the sons of the well-to-do.

Then, as now, the professional classes could afford to take time off work, contribute to the cost of running the club and pay their share of the travelling expenses. If the manager of a company wanted to go on tour for weeks on end, he could easily fit it in with his annual holidays or his sick leave entitlement. The worker on the shop-floor, though, had his pay docked for every minute he was away from his machine.

Rugby union was a game that had wide appeal. In the northern towns, its hard, physical nature and the enjoyment of spending an hour or two in the bar having a drink with other club players appealed to the working-class. Before long, the rugby union clubs in the north of England were among the most successful in the country. County championships were won alternately by Lancashire and Yorkshire; Wigan, St Helens, Leeds and Wakefield were among the most revered sides in the country.

Several clubs in the north in the 1890s, however, found themselves at loggerheads with the administration of the Rugby Football Union (RFU)

Rugby school, the home of all rugby.

based in the south. Some were suspended for compensating their players for loss of wages, and the whole question of compensation for 'broken time' became a bone of contention in the union.

In an effort to stamp out 'broken time' payments, the union, most notably through the influence on the southern clubs, decided to strengthen the regulations covering it. Needless to say, the debate degenerated into class war, the relics of which can still be seen in the antagonism that exists between the Rugby League (RL) and the RFU.

The matter came to a head on 29 August 1895 when a group of representatives from the northern clubs met in the George Hotel, Huddersfield, to draw up separatist plans. By 3 September, the rebels had set up a Northern Rugby Football Union, with twenty-two clubs in membership. The decision was taken with a heavy heart, but the northern clubs felt that, unless they forced the matter, their members would never be able to satisfy both their own players nor the union's officials. It was a bold decision: as the *Wigan Observer* described it at the time . . . 'the freedom from the thraldom of southern gentry was the best thing that could happen.'

The rebels

The 20 clubs that took the decision to pull out of the Rugby Union and set up their own body in 1895 were: Batley, Bradford, Brighouse Rangers, Broughton Rangers, Halifax, Huddersfield, Hull, Hunslet, Leeds, Leigh, Liversedge, Manningham, Oldham, Rochdale Hornets, St Helens, Tyldesley, Wakefield, Warrington, Widnes and Wigan.

Later, Runcorn and Stockport were admitted to membership, so that 22 clubs started the first season. Only one club in the 21 that were represented at

History and development/2

the meeting in the George Hotel in Huddersfield declined to join the new league. That was Dewsbury, but the club changed its mind and began playing against the others in 1898–9.

The number of clubs reached eighty within two years of the inauguration of the Northern Union. Professionalism as such did not begin until 1898, although even then it was decreed by the game's new administrators that no one should earn his living out of the game, a 'working clause' being introduced that demanded that all players should have 'full-time employment'.

The uninformed might assume that the new Northern Rugby Union rushed into full-blown professionalism, the clubs becoming a travelling circus. Far from it. The new Northern Union insisted that players were paid only genuine expenses for 'broken time'. All players had to have full-time jobs in order to qualify for such payments and the limit was just six shillings per appearance.

Neither was the Northern Union an overnight success. Initially tied to the laws of the RFU, the breakaway clubs found difficulty keeping going without the attraction of top-class southern opposition and dwindling crowds meant falling revenue. Gradually pressure grew for change to produce a faster game and a more attractive spectacle. The Challenge Cup (begun in 1896–7) and the alteration of the scoring rule (1897) helped, as did eventually the abolition of line-outs, rucks and mauls.

Open professionalism was not allowed until 1898–9, and not until 1901–2 did a league of Lancashire and Yorkshire clubs form. In 1905, the league, which had previously been split into two, was amalgamated into one, with a Championship Cup introduced as a prize for the top team. In 1906–7 the first major change came: the number of players had been re-

duced to thirteen (a proposal to cut the number to twelve was tried and discarded). Dispensing with wing-forwards brought a more open game, scrum halves and stand-off halves now having room to run with the ball.

The ten years before the First World War saw a rapid expansion into Wales (six clubs joined), although this fizzled out because of the high travelling expenses involved. League also went overseas, with the introduction of the game to New Zealand and Australia, although the game did not reach France until 1934.

Hull of the Northern Union in 1895. They were the first Hull team to grace the Boulevard and this photograph, which was kindly loaned by Mr J. A. Saville, was taken before a match against Liversedge on 21 September 1895.

Although Australia is now one of the strongest nations in the rugby league world, the game began first in New Zealand. A. H. Baskerville, who toured with a New Zealand rugby union side in 1905, was so impressed by the northern game that he set up a squad of what were later called the 'All Golds'. They toured Britain in 1907 and other exhibition games played in Sydney were so successful that they inspired the Australians to form their own rugby league, which toured England in 1908–9 and received an England touring side the following year.

Strangely, however, the game has not, until recent times, caught on in the English south or midlands. A club formed at Coventry lasted only two seasons (1910–11 and 1912–13). Between the wars, there were attempts to start the game south of Watford, but Acton and Willesden (1935–6) lasted one season, Streatham and Mitcham (1935–6 and 1936–7) two. Welsh clubs have come and gone, too, with Pontypridd the only one formed between the wars (1927–8) lasting a season. Cardiff, formed in 1951–2, could survive

History and development/3

only seventeen home matches, the last of which they lost to Wigan by 59–14.

In the last few years, however, rugby league has caught on in England outside the traditional territories. Fulham, the most successful, drew crowds averaging more than 6,000 in their first season (1980–81), after which they were promoted to the first division. Cardiff City, despite their poor attendance record, have settled in the middle of the second division within two seasons of their foundation in 1981–2. Significantly, both Cardiff and Fulham share their grounds with football clubs.

The Rugby League has approved an application from Kent Invicta, who share a ground with Maidstone United in the second division in 1983–4.

Ground-sharing has helped clubs trim their expenses, so that those with gates of only about 3,000 can still afford to pay their players respectable appearance money. It is common practice for players to be paid £40 per match, plus another £40 win bonus. Clubs like Doncaster and Huyton, in particular, whose attendances have been in the hundreds rather than thousands for the last five years, still keep going because hardly any player gets enough money out of the game to live on it. Whereas in Australia, players are paid what amounts to a salary, in the places where it all began, money is tight.

Compared with soccer clubs, who pay their players phenomenal wages and who are forever complaining about their cash-flow problems, rugby league clubs are remarkably robust financially wherever the game is played. A few clubs, such as Fulham, have player sponsorship schemes and lotteries to help with finances, but most keep going purely because their outgoings are so small.

Clearly, changes in the laws, among them the six-tackle rule, have helped keep the crowds coming. Indeed, the early modifications, such as the abolition of wing-forwards and line-outs, kept the game alive in the early years of this century. The changes being introduced now are unlikely to have such a dramatic effect.

Upgrading the value of a try from three to four points, for instance, due to take place in the 1983–4 season is unlikely to tansform the game. David Howes, who looks after the promotion of the game in Britain, believes that it will make little or no difference as to who wins — only to the margin of a victory.

'If you look down previous score-sheets, and adjust the value of a try to four points, you will find that remarkably few results would be altered, only the winning margin,' he says. He cites the example of what happened when the drop goal was devalued to one point in 1973–4. The initial reaction was not to try to drop at goal, but over the last few years the number of drop goals has grown and grown, as players grasp the chance of an extra point or two.

One significant change, however, is the formation of the scrum in 1983–4. The effect should make scrums less of a lottery and favour the 'non-offending side' — more of that in the next section. One of the most frequent criticisms of league is that most scrums are 'a mess'. If the new law on scrummaging tightens that up, the crowds may be drawn back to the game yet again.

Sunday play

For most of the Rugby League's life, the game has been played on Saturdays, with occasional mid-week games. In the early 1970s, however, the league took a bold decision to move the usual match-day to a Sunday.

The move was inspired by the then

The third international touring team to Australia in 1920. The national side was not known as Great Britain until after the Second World War. Photograph by courtesy of Mr J. A. Saville.

secretary, Bill Fallowfield, who considered that Saturday was rapidly becoming a day when people preferred to play golf, go shopping and visit garden centres, rather than travel to matches. Sunday was becoming the day for watching sport, he believed, and how right he turned out to be. As crowds have drifted away from the Saturday-based sports, the attendances at rugby league grounds have held up well.

But before Sunday could become a rugby league day, the clubs had to overcome resistance from the various factions in the community that wanted to keep Sundays non-commercial. This was achieved in two ways: by selling programmes for the game rather than take money for entrance alone; and some grounds had a 'free gate', a place where anyone could enter without payment. Needless to say, many rugby league clubs would have gone broke quickly if the locations of their 'free gate' were well-known. At Hull, for instance, the 'free gate' still exists, but is almost impossible to find.

Rules/1

Rugby league pitches vary in size and inclination, but they all fall within dimensions specified by the Rugby League. The pitch is never wider than 68 metres, nor longer than 122 metres (including the in-goal area, which can be anything from 6 to 11 metres deep).

So when a player runs the length of the pitch to score a try, he is covering roughly 100 metres. In doing so, he will pass the half-way line and two lines 22 metres from the try-lines at each end. If he keeps well infield, he may also pass six dotted lines, three in each half of the field. The first is the 10 metre line, which is 10 metres from the goal line; the second is 10 metres past the 22 and the third is 10 metres from half-way.

In the centre of the goal-line is the goal, which traditionally is H-shaped, but which could, according to the laws, be shaped like a tuning fork, with just one pole supporting the cross-bar. In any event, the cross-bar has to be three metres off the ground and 5.5 metres long. There are also lines 10 metres from each touchline.

The ball is oval, air-inflated and is of leather or other approved material. It is between 27 and 29 centimetres long. The weight when the ball is clean and dry is between 380 gram and 440 gram — but when wet it weighs a ton!

Scoring points

The object of the game is to score points, and the quickest way of amassing them is to score tries. Traditionally, the try is worth three points, although it is to be increased to four from the 1983–4 season. A try is scored when a player from the attacking team places the ball on the goal-line or within the in-goal area and exerts downward pressure on it with his hand (or part of his body).

Having scored a try, a team is allowed to appoint a member to take a place-kick at goal, which counts as two points if it clears the crossbar and passes between the uprights, or a theoretically infinite vertical extension of the uprights. The attempt is judged by the touch-judges, who stand behind the posts when the kick is being taken and indicate the scoring of the goal by raising their flags. A goal-kick taken after a try is scored must be taken from the same distance from touch as the point where the try was scored.

Points can also be scored by penalty kicks. These are place-kicks taken by the non-offending team from the point where the offending team has committed a serious breach of the laws. If successful, these also merit two points. The only other way of scoring is a drop goal, which can be attempted from any part of the field. A player in possession will drop the ball at his feet and kick it as it rebounds (on the 'half-volley'). If the ball passes over the opponent's crossbar and between the uprights, as judged by the referee, the team scores one point.

In the event of an infringement being committed after a try has been scored, the referee is empowered to award a 'seven-point try'. This means that, in addition to the first goal-kick, the side that scores can take a second kick at goal from in front of the posts — yielding seven points if the two goals are added to the original three for a try. (In 1983–4, when the value of the try becomes four points, it is an 'eight-point try').

Each team has 13 players, and may use two substitutes, who themselves may be substituted for up to a maximum of four substitutions. A substitute may not, however, be brought on simply to kick at goal.

The start

The match starts with a place-kick from the centre of the half-way line,

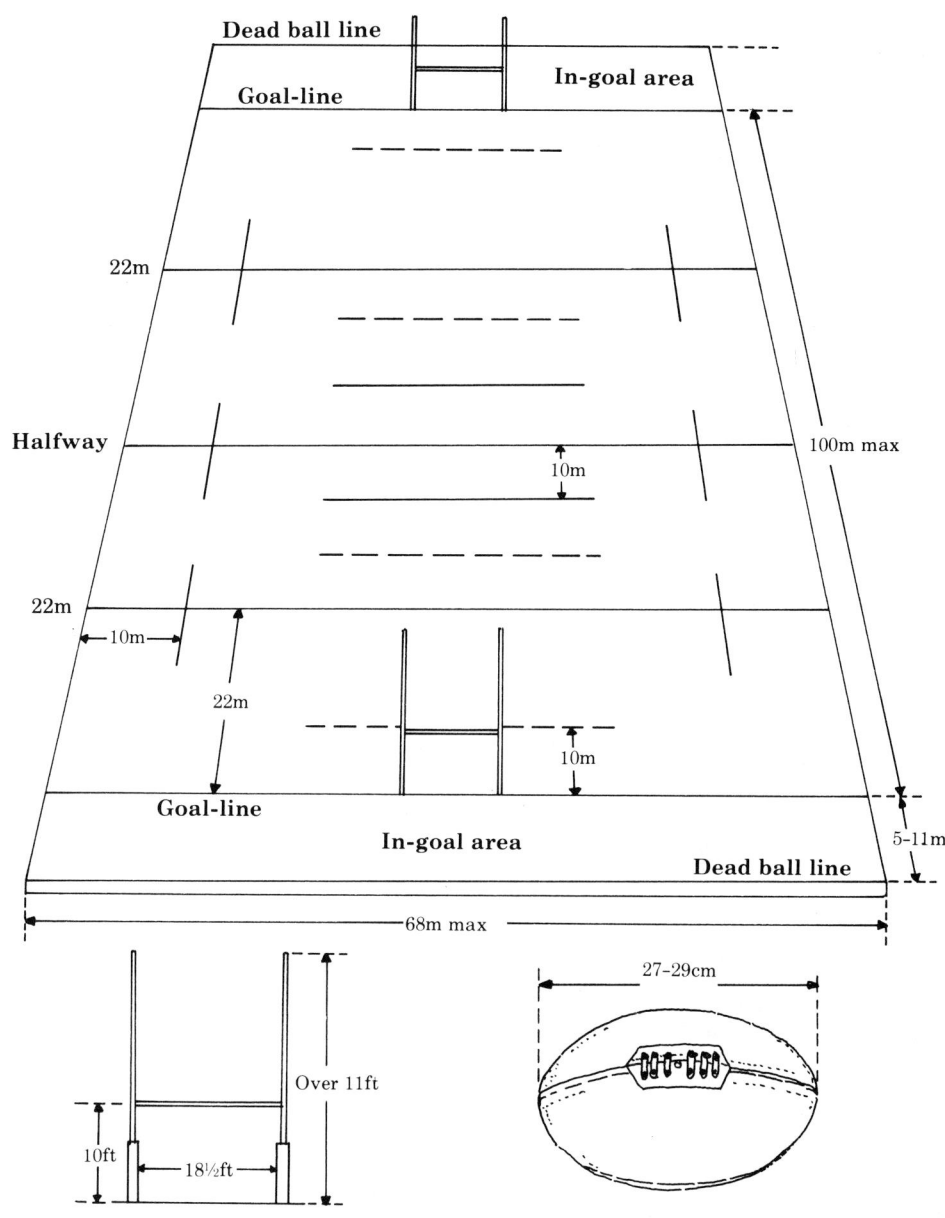

The goals are traditionally H-shaped, but could be shaped like a tuning fork with one pole supporting the cross-bar, which must be 3m off the ground and 5.5m long.

The ball is oval and weighs between 380 grams and 440 grams — that is, when the weather is dry!

15

Rules/2

the kick being taken by the team that loses the toss for choice of ends. Play can also be restarted with a place kick from the 22-metre line by the defending side if an attacking player last touched the ball before it went of play over the dead-ball line or touch-in goal, other than after a penalty kick; or when an attacking player accidentally infringes in the goal area or is tackled in the in-goal area before he grounds the ball.

Opposing players must retire 10 metres from the 22, and should not advance until the ball is kicked. A deliberate offence by either side results in a penalty at the centre of the 22.

The play can also restart with a 'drop out' after an unsuccessful penalty kick has been taken and the ball goes 'dead'. The kick is taken from the centre of the 22. There is also provision for restarting the game from the centre of the goal-line if:
a defending player last touched the ball before it went 'dead' or into touch-in-goal;
a defending player has accidentally infringed behind his own goal line;
a defending player touches down in the in-goal area;
a defending player kicks the ball into touch on the full from his own in-goal;
the ball or a defending player touches the officials or an encroaching spectator in the in-goal area.

The tackle

There are no rucks or mauls in rugby league — these are the loose scrums that frequently form in rugby union with the ball on the ground (ruck) or in a player's hands (maul). Once a player is tackled (and if there is any doubt, the referee shouts 'held' to indicate that he considers the tackle has been completed). Both players should get up again immediately and the player in possession normally places the ball at his feet (known as play-the-ball) and heels it to a player behind him (known as the dummy-half or acting half-back) who will then distribute it as he feels fit.

When the ball is placed on the ground (in front of the tackled player's foremost foot) any player can technically kick it in any direction, but raising a foot above the ground before the ball is released by the tackled player results in a penalty being awarded against the offender. All players other than the two taking part in the play-the-ball and the two acting half-backs are penalised if they fail to retire five yards behind their own player taking part in the play-the-ball or behind their own goal line. As soon as the ball is released by the tackled player, the other players may advance.

Technically, it is illegal to 'steal the ball' in the tackle, although it is permissable to do so provided the tackle has not been completed. A recent change in the laws allows the tackle to progress until such time as the tackled player's momentum has been stopped. This has led to some confusion as to when the tackle has been completed, and puts the onus on referees to shout 'held' (or sometimes 'play on') when they consider the tackle is completed.

Once play has started, any player who is onside or in play can run with the ball, kick it in any direction and throw or knock it in any direction other than towards his opponents' goal line (unless it is as a result of charging down a kick by an opponent). Any player who is holding the ball may be tackled. He can be shoulder-charged, but only if he and his opponent are both running towards a loose ball.

If the ball goes into touch, a scrum is ordered ten metres in-field from the place where the ball went out of play. Up to the end of the 1982–3 season, the attacking team has had the loose head

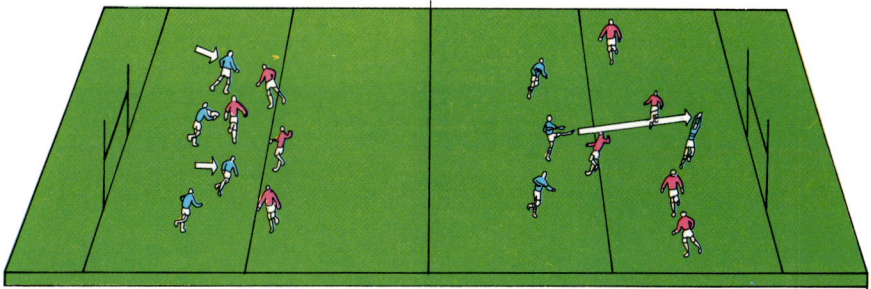

Offside A   **Offside B**

The scrum

The tackle

The scrum: This happens after six tackles or when the ball goes into touch or for certain offences. From the 1983-4 season the non-offending side has the put-in and the loose head.

The tackle: Once a player is tackled the players must get up. The referee decides whether a tackle is made.

Rules/3

in the scrum and the defending team put the ball in. However, the laws are being changed to give the loose head and the put-in to the non-offending side.

Offences

Most offences in the game — such as a knock-on or a forward pass — warrant a scrum, which is also what happens when the side with the ball is tackled six times. More serious infringments — such as tackling without the ball, dangerous play and offside — lead to a penalty kick awarded to the non-offending side. In these cases, the non-offending side can choose to kick at goal or, if such a kick is difficult or out of range of the posts, to kick to touch — and then start the game again with a 'tap' penalty from a point ten metres in from where their first kick went into touch.

There is also a device known as a differential penalty or free-kick which the referee can award when he spots a 'technical' infringement — such as not putting the ball into the scrum correctly or striking for the ball in the scrum before the ball is thrown in by the scrum half. The referee indicates a differential penalty by waving his outstretched arm up-and-down whilst signalling a penalty. The side awarded a differential penalty is not allowed to kick at goal, but can kick for touch and restart with a tap penalty ten metres from where the ball went out of play.

Offside is an offence often misunderstood by the viewer. A player is offside if the ball is kicked, touched or held by one of his own side behind him, unless he is in his own in-goal area. An offside player is not allowed to take part in the game or attempt to influence its course until he is onside again. He is not allowed to encroach within five metres of an opponent who is waiting for the ball, and must immediately retire five metres from any opponent who first secures possession.

Offside players are put onside if an opponent moves five metres with the ball; if the opponent touches the ball without retaining it; if a player on his own side who has the ball runs in front of him; if one of his own side kicks the ball and takes up a position in front of him; or if he retires behind a point where the ball was last touched by one of his own side.

In rugby league, players who kick or knock the ball into touch on the full, from any part of the pitch do not gain advantage and a scrum forms from the point where the ball was last kicked or touched. Hence players try to kick the ball along the ground into touch to gain ground.

What you would reasonably expect to be foul play — such as trampling on opponents, tackling too high and dangerous kicking — is penalised heavily in rugby league. Not only are penalties awarded but the offenders can be sent off, either temporarily (into the dressing room, or 'sin bin') or for the rest of the game. Referees never shirk their responsibilities in this area of the law and will despatch a player to the dressing-room without hesitation if they see something nasty going on. They are tougher on miscreants than referees or umpires in almost any other sport and are intimidated by no one. They normally have the full backing of the authorities and the clubs concerned for their decisions.

On the right, a scrum shapes up to go down (1); play-the-ball (2) is demonstrated by Featherstone in the 1983 Wembley cup final and (3) a referee awards a penalty kick.

Rules/4

Keeping time

The time is kept by an official time-keeper, who sounds a hooter at the start and end of the game, which finishes at the first stoppage after the hooter has blown — unless a try has been scored or a penalty is awarded, in which case an attempt at goal is permitted outside normal time. The referee signals to the time-keeper to stop the clock to allow for an injured player to be treated, if play has to be halted for such treatment to take place.

Referees

Referees in rugby league do not mince words when controlling a game and one of the characteristics of their style is the clarity with which they announce their decisions. Signals to players (and to the crowd) are so emphatic and positive that there is hardly ever any dissension.

If a player is heard to mumble about a refereeing decision, the man with the whistle will promptly move ten metres nearer to the offending player's goal-line and award the penalty from there instead. Referees like Fred Lindop — considered by many to be the best referee in the league — never leave any room for doubt. That they are so demonstrative when they announce their decisions is no accident, for one of the most basic rules of rugby league refereeing is that the public and the players should be kept fully informed of decisions as and when they are made.

There is now a drive by the RL to make referees fitter than ever to encourage them to be on top-form throughout the season. Moreover, referees are not frightened of constructive criticism: under the rules, the host club is entitled to invite the official into the boardroom after the game and raise any queries with him in private — all with the aim of improving the understanding on both sides.

There are standard signals which the referee has to adopt in indicating why he has given a particular decision, and these are written down in the laws of the game. In fact the role of the referee a century ago was to arbitrate between two touch-judges. The touch-judges waved their flags to indicate their decision; in the event of disagreement between the two, the referee would blow on his whistle as a kind of casting vote, showing which touch-judge he agreed with.

Nowadays, the duties of a touch-judge are to indicate where a ball has gone out of play and, for a penalty, to indicate how far back the offending team should stand at the restart; to signify a goal having been scored or an attempt having failed; and to draw the referee's attention to an offence that has occurred on the field that the referee himself may not have seen, in which case the touch-judge enters the field of play waving his flag. The referee can accept or reject the touch-judge's evidence as he sees fit.

Rugby league referees are masters of 'man management'. More often than not, a 16-stone second row forward can be put in his place by a referee half his size. Not surprisingly, the whole weight of the Rugby League and often the club itself is behind the referee in his bid to keep what can be a hard physical game clean and fair.

The sin-bin was introduced at the start of the 1982–3 season as a method of censuring players who were guilty of a serious misdemeanour on the field but whose offence did not warrant sending off. The referee will order a player to return to the dressing-room for a fixed period — usually ten minutes but sometimes five. The penalty period is indicated by the number of fingers the referee raises in the air when he sends the player from the

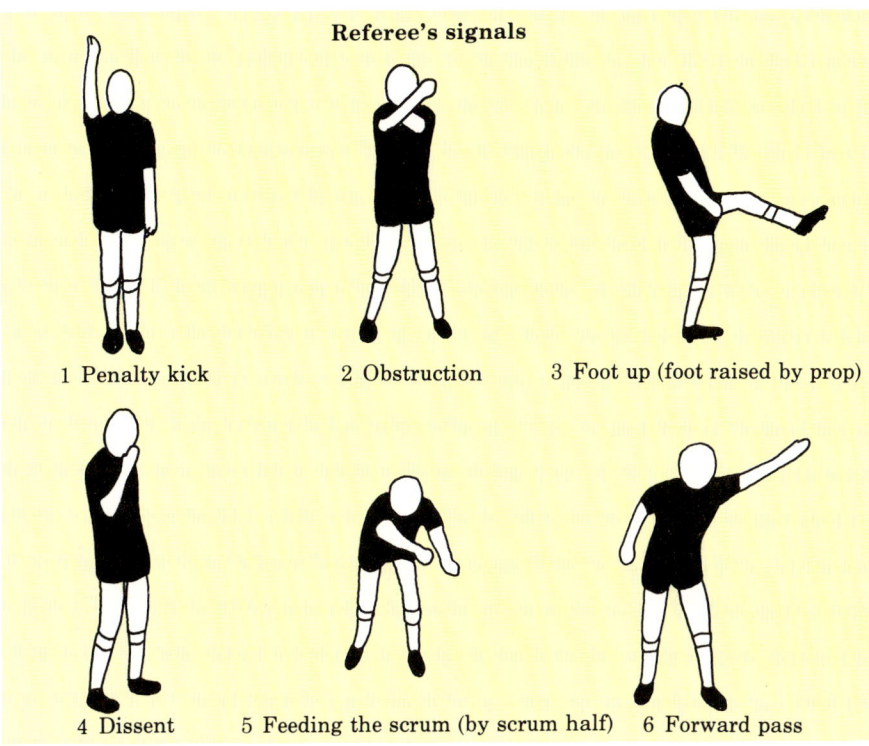

Referee's signals

1 Penalty kick
2 Obstruction
3 Foot up (foot raised by prop)
4 Dissent
5 Feeding the scrum (by scrum half)
6 Forward pass

field.

It is a controversial measure and it is too early to assess its effect on players' conduct. Those who have been ordered off the field for a fixed time make light of it: a chance to have a rest (one ex-Fulham player claimed he was able to finish off the pre-match bottle of sherry while in the sin-bin, and thereby felt much warmer when he returned).

If a referee sends a player off for the rest of the game, then he is required by law to file a report to the Rugby League and to the club explaining his reasons and the player may face disciplinary charges as a result. Hence the sin-bin can be seen as a convenient way of removing an angry or careless individual from the playing area, giving him time to 'cool off' and then readmitting him without the need to write reports afterwards and without any long term effect on the player's career.

There are others who believe that the only way of stamping out dangerous play is to bring down the full weight of authority on the offenders and to ram the point home by banning them from one or two games afterwards — thereby hitting their wallets as well as their pride. Doubtless the International Board will keep a close check on the sin-bin experiment.

Losing a player does not necessarily have a bad effect on a team's performance. Experience shows that 12 men who have to cover for a missing player are far more diligent in defence and try even harder to plug the gap that their missing member has left.

The Stars

Rugby league is full of personalities, characters who over the years have delighted the crowds and the viewers with their performances on and off the field. League has suffered a little because of its parochial origins, and has not had the national coverage it deserved, but those who have been watching the game since the Second World War have been treated to a feast of enjoyment provided by a host of outstanding individuals.

Reg Bowden (Fulham)

When Reg Bowden signed for Fulham before their inaugural 1980–1 season, many thought that he was fast approaching the end of his playing career as he could see no future for himself in the cut-and-thrust of first division football at Widnes. He was aged 30 at the time, and he had been playing in the top flight since 1968.

Worse still, it seemed, he was a scrum-half who had been harrassed and battered in no fewer than 16 major cup finals. However, Bowden confounded his critics to such an extent that, three seasons later, he willingly signed a new three-year contract with the London club and no one was left in any doubt that he was one of the most outstanding scrum-halves and inspirational leaders in the game.

Bowden's role at Fulham soon became that of player-coach: his wide experience and ability to read and understand the game made him the most important figure at Craven Cottage through those first three turbulent seasons — when Fulham were promoted, then relegated, and took the second division title in 1982–3. He has dropped himself from the team when his fitness is in doubt and so given Tony Kinsey, a young utility player, a chance to prove himself. He has returned to the side at regular intervals to guide and support his team. There seems little doubt that Bowden will continue to make a significant contribution to the game for some years yet.

Lee Crooks (Hull)

A name to watch in the second half of the 1980s must be Lee Crooks of Hull. A second-row forward who is not far off 15-stone, Crooks had an outstanding 1982–3 season. He played a major part in bringing his side the first division championship by scoring 200 points for the club; he won caps in the two of the three Dominion Insurance Test matches between Great Britain and Australia; and he forced Featherstone to concede a try that very nearly brought Hull the cup at Wembley in May.

All that in a season, and yet Crooks was only 19 years old. Not surprisingly, Crooks is now the youngest-ever forward to make his first appearance for Great Britain. Even so, he could not stand in the way of the all-conquering Australian tourists. Another 10 years experience, however, and Crooks could well be a name as famous as any the rugby league has yet produced.

The Stars/2

Des Drummond (Leigh)

Not surprisingly, backs always appeal to the spectator, as Leigh's Des Drummond has found. He was a regular try-scorer for the Lancashire side, delighting the crowd with his pace and determination on the wing. Then the television-sponsored *Superstars* competition put his face on the screen and he became a household name, winning the national finals and following in the footsteps of that other rugby league Superstar, Keith Fielding.

In France, Drummond has been dubbed the 'Black Prince'. A product of Leigh's colts system, Drummond is Jamaican-born. Few need reminding of his speed off the mark and his fitness. In his activities off-the-field, Drummond broke the record for the fastest 100 metres and in the gym tests in the 1983 *Superstars* competition.

Despite his elevation to folk-hero, Drummond retains his soft northern accent and his cheery smile, which makes him popular wherever Leigh or Great Britain play. He has been voted the most outstanding winger in the world and is regularly among the leading try-scorers in the league.

Steve Fenwick (Cardiff City)

Steve Fenwick, like David Watkins his team manager, took less than two seasons to make the transition from top-flight rugby union player to international rugby league. A centre who is fast and elusive in broken play, Fenwick is also one of the most reliable kickers in the game, and almost always rises to the big occasion.

Usually, it takes fully three seasons for a union player to fit into the league, and some never make the grade at all.

Fenwick has used all the ball-skills he learned in the valleys of South Wales and applied them to the professional game. This 12st 8lb centre, formerly of Bridgend, Wales and the British Lions, is expected to remain with Cardiff City for some years to come and played a key role in his side's surprisingly-comprehensive victory over the second division champions Fulham in Cardiff's final match in their disappointing 1982–3 campaign.

Stamford Bridge is the unusual setting for rugby league, in this case between Cardiff and Fulham in 1983.

The Stars/3

Roger Millward (HKR)

The greatest British player ever to take the field since the war is arguably Roger Millward, now manager of the successful Hull Kingston Rovers side. Millward's road to the top was not an easy one and during his first two seasons with Castleford he was forever being relegated to the second team because Alan Hardisty and Keith Hepworth, both Test players in the 1960s, were occupying the two half-back positions.

Millward saw his chance, however, to gain experience of first division football in 1966, when Castleford agreed to his transfer to Hull KR for a fee of £6,000. He was to make more than 400 appearances in the Hull KR jersey, scoring 207 tries (a record for the club) and 564 goals in his 14 seasons there.

Millward retired from playing after his jaw was broken for the fourth time in an A-team match against Batley in 1980. But that did not end his involvement in the game, for he was appointed coach to Hull KR and later manager.

His clever reading of the game and speed near the goal-line were remarkable and he more than deserved his 29 caps over 12 years for Great Britain — he was captain 10 times. Indeed, in the second Test in Sydney against Australia in 1970 he equalled the best match total by a British player against Australia with no fewer than seven goals and two tries. What also made Millward stand out was that he played international rugby in four different positions: stand-off, scrum half, centre and wing.

Having retired from playing, Millward is still keen to see the advancement of the game. He says: 'The game has changed a great deal since I started playing in 1962-3. The old ideas were still there when i first took the field, but the playing styles have now altered, and fitness levels are much higher. It's a little more difficult to score tries now, but I expect that someone will someday beat my record at Hull KR. Records are there to be broken, after all.'

The Stars/4

Steve Quinn (Featherstone Rovers)

Steve Quinn wrote a little piece of Wembley history when he kicked a crucial penalty goal in the 1983 Challenge cup final to take his side Featherstone Rovers to a 14–12 win over Hull, who were clear favourites. It was the biggest upset in years. Before the match, the bookmakers were so convinced that Hull would trounce the colliery village side that they were not prepared to offer odds on either team, only on the size of Hull's win.

Yet Quinn's performance — four goals on the day — was not remarkable at all. Then aged 30, this 13-stone centre already held the Featherstone club record for most points in a career (previously held by the legendary Don Fox), despite having joined the club from York only in 1976 — though he scored four goals on his debut for the club. His best season was 1979–8 when he scored 375 points (including 163 goals).

Quinn's direct, no-nonsense approach and his accuracy puts him among the leading goalkickers of all time. He jointly holds the record for the fastest 'century' of goals, secured after just eighteen matches in the 1979–80 season. The other players to have achieved that are Bernard Ganley (1957–8) and David Watkins (1972–3).

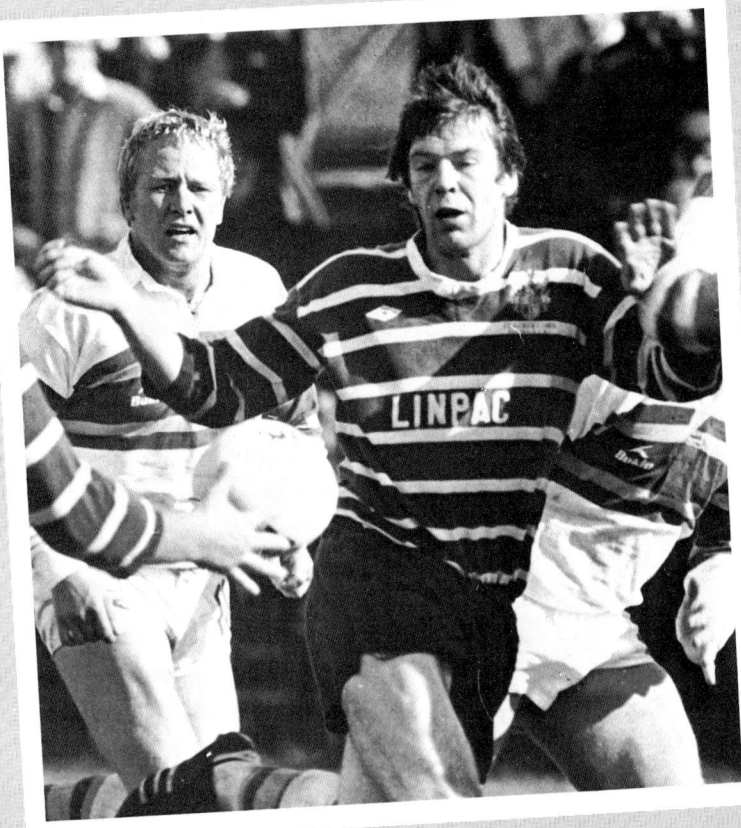

David Hobbs (Featherstone Rovers)

The man who won the Lance Todd trophy as the man-of-the-match in the Wembley Challenge Cup final in 1983 was David Hobbs, then just 24. Not only did he score two superb tries on the day, but the hard tackling and solid workrate of this 15-stone Featherstone Second-row presented Hull with their greatest problem. Already a Great Britain under-24 international, Hobbs is a 'collier' who can kick goals as well as Steve Quinn and scored seven for the national team against France whilst winning his two caps.

Hobbs is undoubtedly a man to watch in the future. It is generally thought that a forward in rugby league does not reach his peak until he is in his later 20s, which means that, at time of writing, Hobbs has another four years before he is at his best. Significantly, he was also top first division try-scorer during the 1981–2 season, using his 6ft 1in to reach no fewer than 19 touch-downs during the campaign. (In 1982–3, the top try scorer was Bob Eccles of Warrington, another forward, which goes to show the increasing fitness and agility expected of the men who are in the game's powerhouse.)

The Stars/5

Club directors

The game goes beyond the players and coaching staff to managing directors and club chairmen, each of whom are characters in themselves. They are very much businessmen. Harold Genders, managing director of Fulham, and Jack Grindrod, chairman of Rochdale Hornets and of the Rugby League, are businessmen determined to make the books balance and to make the game possible. Though they may at times seem hard-nosed, tough individuals who are forever looking for value for money out of their players, they have the best interests of the game at heart: unless the sport shows a decent return on the investment that they put in, it will surely die.

Those who say that the boards of rugby league clubs do not care about the sport and are only interested in it as a money-making device are mistaken. Few rugby league clubs make a profit within five years of their formation, and it takes a sympathetic heart to keep ploughing money in without any sign of a return for that length of time. Directors who have started league clubs in the expectation of recovering their money in the short-term have been sorely disappointed and many have now disappeared from the game altogether.

The latest applicant to join the Rugby League, Kent Invicta, is masterminded by businessman Paul Faires in Maidstone, and he knows full well that unless he sees the new club as a long-term project, it cannot survive. Faires himself has drawn up a five-year plan for the new side, but he is not making any assumptions about early profit.

Harold Genders

Jack Grindrod

David Oxley

At the head of the administration is the secretary of the Rugby League, David Oxley. Hull-born and educated at Oxford, he was selected to take over from Bill Fallowfield. The choice of Oxley was a surprising one in 1974, but, with the benefit of hindsight, it was the right decision. Oxley brought to the league a different style, one that appeals to the regions where the game is expanding. With his academic achievements and his charming manner, Oxley was just the figurehead that league needed to continue its campaign to become a truly national game in Britain. The first fruits of Oxley's new look are just beginning to show, with clubs established in the South of England and Wales and the greater recognition that the game has had at a national level since he took over.

David Howes

Aiding Oxley is David Howes, a journalist who used to work for the Hull *Daily Mail* but who has taken over the public relations activities of the league, which used to be done out-of-house by a PR consultancy. Howes' performance at the league's headquarters in Chapeltown Road, Leeds has been remarkable, not only because there has been a steady flow of information for press and media to bite on, but because Howes has managed to attract substantial sponsorship for the game. The sponsorship has enabled the league to improve facilities at grounds and make the game more attractive to spectators.

David Howes

Road to the top

One of the principal reasons for the hostility between the rugby union and rugby league authorities is the RFU law that any player who has played the professional game, be it rugby league or American grid-iron football (other than in the Armed Forces) is automatically banned for life from playing rugby union again. Traditionally, union players have therefore been approached in the utmost secrecy by scouts from league clubs, usually skulking around corners in Welsh mining villages. The scouts make a take-it-or-leave-it offer to the amateur player and then vanish into the night.

Times have changed a little, but still the approach of a rugby league scout is treated with suspicion and ill-feeling by rugby union die-hards, who fear that their best youngsters will be spirited away from them by the offer of money. As long as there is a shortage of rugby league-trained youngsters the practice of poaching players from the leading union clubs will go on.

David Watkins, formerly of Newport RU, Wales and the British Lions, was one of those approached by Salford to play league — and having accepted the offer he is now banned for life from playing or coaching union. At first, Watkins resisted the temptation to go north, but, when he had done almost everything it was possible to do in the amateur game, he eventually succumbed, joined Salford and promptly achieved national and international honours in the 'professional code'.

Watkins has noticed the difference over the years, however. Now manager of Cardiff City Rugby League Club, he says: 'When I was first approached, it was by a seedy little man in a raincoat who was waiting outside my house. Nowadays, I myself am approached regularly by rugby union players who want to know what it is worth for them to turn league. There is

The ultimate 'front row': left to right, Lord Derby, Jack Grindrod and David Oxley — respectively the president, the 1982-3 chairman and the secretary general of the Rugby League at the unveiling of the £80,000 improvements to Headquarters in Leeds in October 1982.

Road to the top/2

still some hostility among the die-hards, of course, but contact between league clubs and potential recruits are a good deal less furtive than they used to be.'

What has also changed — for the benefit of rugby league — is the education system. Before the introduction of comprehensive schools, Britain had a tri-partite system of state education: grammar, secondary and technical schools. Typically, in the north of England, the grammar school boys played union, the secondary modern school boys played league.

The gradual erosion of the grammar schools over the last ten years has led to a rapid growth of rugby league sides at secondary level. Comprehensive schools in the north of England are favouring league, because it is part of the fabric of the community in the northern mill towns and also because its adherents believe it to be safer. The Rugby League itself is particularly keen on the safety aspect: scrums are rarely trials of strength in league and mauls and rucks do not occur, so reducing the injury toll.

This has led to the growth of the English Schools Rugby League Association, of the Universities and Colleges RL group, and now the body that bridges the gap between school and university, the Upper Schools and Sixth-form Colleges Association (Buscarla). Each of these has helped the game to be available to youngsters from primary school to graduation; it has stopped the need to switch to union in order to get a game at certain ages; and it has helped bring forward rugby league players from their first experience of the game to full-blown professional status.

That process has also reduced the reliance on rugby union clubs as

The top of the tree: Featherstone and Hull in play at Wembley during the 1983 Challenge cup final.

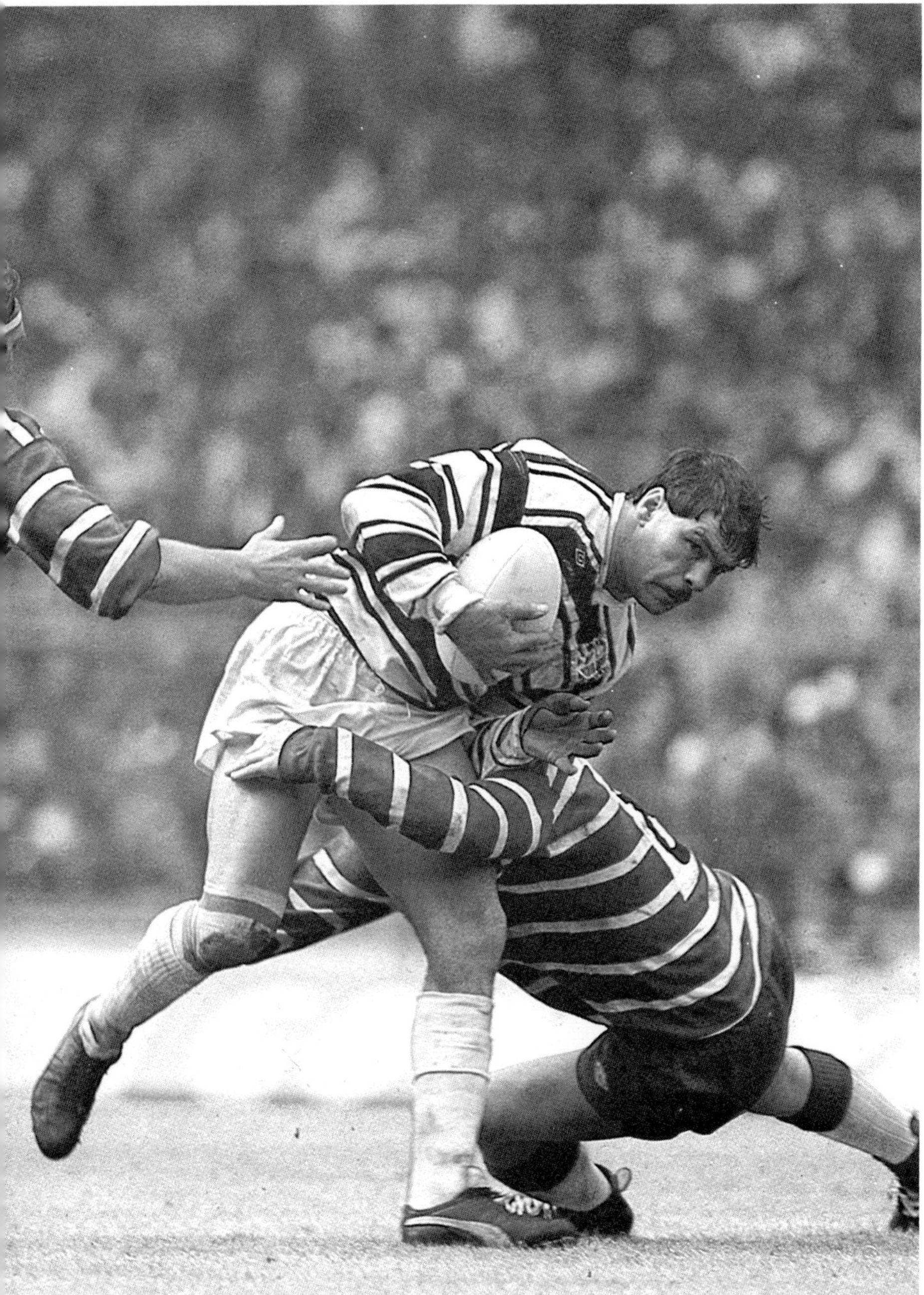

Road to the top/3

places where future rugby league players can learn their basic skills. In a back-handed fashion, it should also reduce the number of players who turn from union to league and find they cannot cope with the professional code. They end up in no-man's land.

Apart from the professional game, there is a thriving amateur game with its own association, the British Amateur Rugby League Association (BARLA), whose administrator is Maurice Oldroyd. One of the most passionate supporters of the game at every level, Oldroyd has seen BARLA grow from a tiny, fledgling organisation not even recognised by the Rugby League itself, to an important institution for the promotion of the game at amateur level, with the full support of Chapeltown Road.

So rugby league has been able to breed its own players, which is just as well because former rugby union players do not always make the grade, and even when they do they often take two or three seasons to master the techniques. Some, like David Watkins and Keith Fielding, make the top-flight in both codes. Watkins had an international career in both codes and Fielding, who played for England at the highest level at union, became a favourite at Salford within a short time of his move. Many others take longer to adjust to the different playing styles. Some even turn to league with the idea that it is a 'soft game' played by padded-up 'thickies' and they get a rude awakening.

Those that progress from the amateur rugby league clubs know what's coming. Martin Herdman, a Fulham second-row forward and one-time professional boxer, learned the game at Peckham, one of the leading London amateur sides, and he has not looked back since, providing the power to the Craven Cottage club's 'engine room'.

Recruits: some players graduate from rugby union, such as Keith Fielding. Others start younger, like this small Dewsbury fan.

Cups and competitions

Competition is the essence of rugby league. Remarkably few matches in a league season are 'friendlies' and only when these are linked to a special occasion do they pull in large crowds (one of the largest at Fulham, however, was a 'challenge' match between the London side and Bradford Northern at the end of the 1980-1 season, although one reason 12,000 people were attracted to Craven Cottage was that it was held on the eve of the Challenge Cup final at Wembley).

The four leading competitions in the league are the championship, sponsored by the Slalom Lager group, for which the top side in each of the two divisions receives a trophy; the premiership, for which the top eight teams in the first division play-off at the end of each season; the John Player Trophy; and most celebrated of all the Challenge Trophy, sponsored by the State Express cigarette company, which has its final at Wembley each May.

Competitions are crucial to the survival of rugby league, as the Northern Union discovered at the turn of the century, when the Challenge Cup and leagues were started in a bid to revive flagging interest in the game. That is because many games have a special significance. One problem with the present league championship system is that clubs in the bottom half of each table suffer falling gates because they have little left to fight for: they are neither in danger of relegation, nor do they stand any chance of winning the championship trophy.

Attempts to improve that situation, though, have met with difficulty. Once, in the mid-1960s, the Rugby League began a 'top 16' play-off for the championshjip trophy, and a 'bottom 14' play-off for another trophy in an effort to provide some extra interest for the mediocre teams. Not surprisingly, the 'bottom 14' play-off hardly

The Challenge cup: Featherstone celebrate victory at Wembley in 1983.

Cups and competitions/2

got off the ground.

Promotion and relegation provides a major interest among crowds. The system of four-up, four-down seems to work well in a two-division system that has been running since 1973–4. Unlike football, there is no 'European' qualification for, say, the fifth and sixth-placed first division teams to fight for, but so unpredictable are rugby league results that it is rare for a team to run away with the title by February or March, and so there is always a battle almost to the end of the season for the championship trophy.

The Challenge Cup, which is played on a single-match, knock-out basis, has throughout its history been the most coveted trophy of all. The final has been at Wembley since 1929 and even with full television coverage draws a crowd in excess of 90,000 to the capital. Challenge Cup matches rarely run to form and the frequent 'upsets' provide extra spice.

The competition attracts enormous sponsorship. In 1982–3, the fifth season of State Express sponsorship, the tobacco company put a record £110,000 into the tournament. Of that, £70,000 was prize money, the winners receiving £14,555 and the runners-up £8,000. The remaining £40,000 went into the Rugby League's Capital Development Fund to improve grounds and facilities of clubs in membership.

The 1983 final proved to be the day of the underdog. Unfancied Featherstone Rovers caused a great surprise by beating Hull, who had already won the Slalom Lager league championship. Hull went on to lose the premiership final to Widnes, who thus became the first club to win outside the top four finishers in the league. In fact the league winners have never won the premiership title.

The choice of Wembley, considered by the Rugby League to be the boldest

Wembley: Hull and Hull KR players salute their fans before the start of the 1980 final.

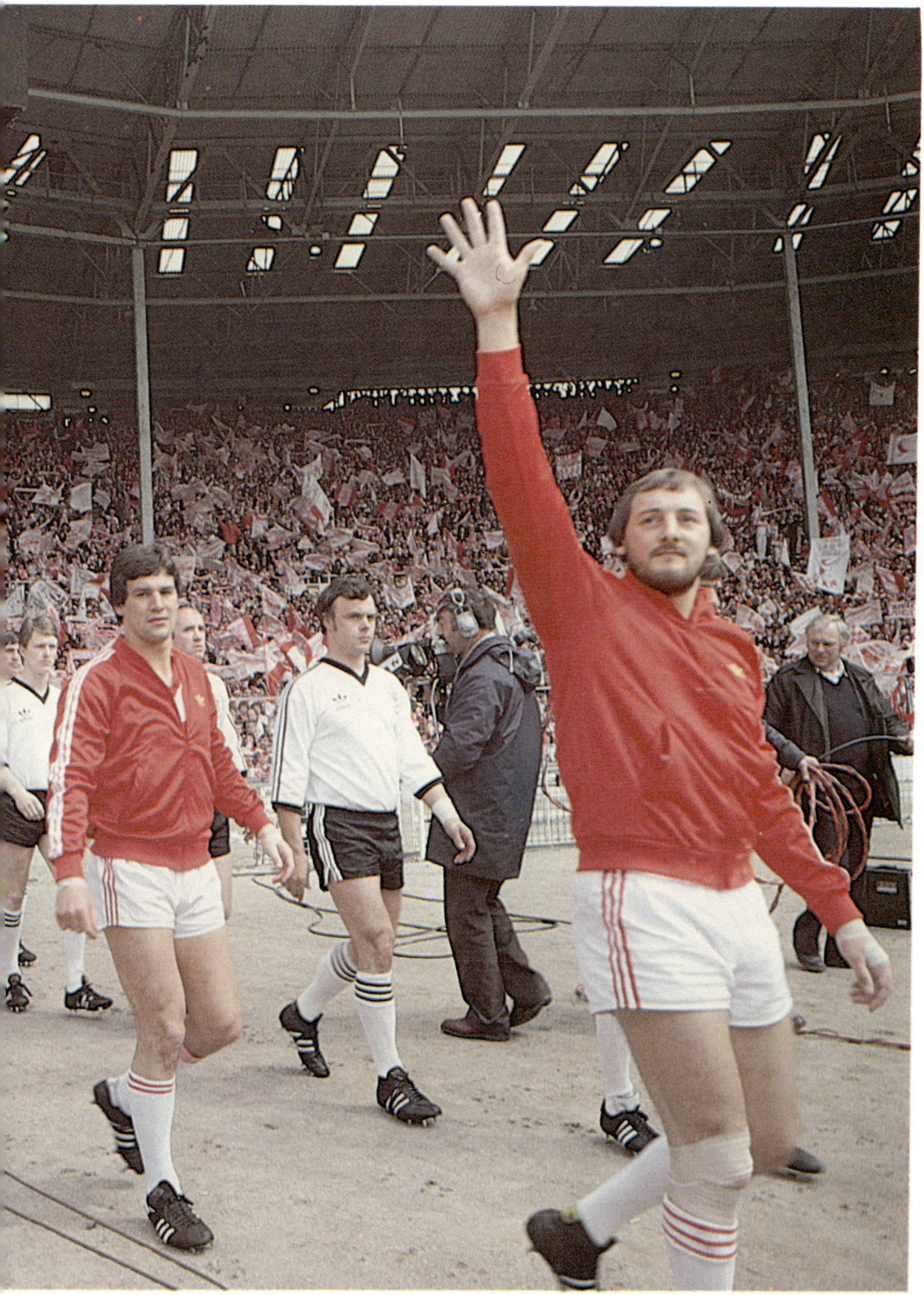

Cups and competitions/3

step it has ever made, was an astonishing departure for the northern clubs, but by far the most sensible one they ever made, for it brought the game national coverage in the media. The Rugby League has not been slow to make the occasion into a festival, with marching bands, schoolboy curtain-raiser matches and community singing. Three times, Wembley has been full to bursting point, with crowds of over 90,000 attending. Rarely are there many empty spaces in the stadium, despite 'live' television coverage.

At the Wembley final, a trophy is awarded to the player who in the opinion of members of the Rugby League Writers Association, has made the most outstanding performance. The Lance Todd trophy, instituted in 1946, commemorates a New Zealand player who first came to Britain with a touring party of Kiwis in 1907, who subsequently played for Wigan and Dewsbury and became manager of Salford. After he was killed in a car crash, a group of leading figures in the league set up a fund to provide the trophy and a replica for the winner. Sponsorship of this award has been augmented more recently by Greenall Whitley, the brewers.

The choice of the leading player in the Wembley final sometimes mystifies viewers, who, having seen the game, would have nominated another. Often the journalists in the Wembley press box are divided in their opinion as to who has contributed most to the final itself, particularly as they are asked to vote on the issue before the end of the first hour of the Wembley game. They tend to take into account the performance of players not just in the final but in the semi-finals, both of which most rugby

John Player trophy: The Wigan captain, Colin Whitfield, with the spoils of victory in January 1983 (top) and the Headingley ground, Leeds, before the kick-off. The trophy, which is the first of the major open cup finals, used to be known as Players No 6 trophy until 1977-8.

43

Cups and competitions/4

league writers will have seen as the two semi-finals are traditionally played on separate Saturdays. Hence the award of the trophy is an appreciation of not only what a player has done in the final but of the effect he had on bringing his side to Wembley beforehand.

The other major knock-out trophy is the John Player Competition, also sponsored by a tobacco company. Formerly known as the Player's No 6 Trophy, the tournament is contested in the first half of the season by the professional clubs and the leading amateur sides. The introduction of the leading amateur clubs has given the minnows a chance to take on the professionals, but an upset, though not unknown, is rare. The final always takes place at a ground in the north.

There are also county competitions, the Lancashire and Yorkshire Cup, for which the professional clubs compete in the early part of the season. These are sponsored by Forshaws and Webster's breweries respectively.

Sponsorship

Until relatively recent times, sponsorship was not a matter of much concern to the Rugby League authorities. That all changed with the appointment of David Oxley as general secretary in 1973 and David Howes, the league's first full-time public relations officer, in 1974. Howes, in particular, is interested in bringing corporate money into the game for the well-being of those involved in it, but with this difference: he is concerned that money is attracted for the long-term benefit of the sport and that the game does not become wholly dependent on it.

His policy has proved a resounding success. So far, more than £400,000 has been attracted each season for a host of events much of it being in the form of prize money, but a significant

The international scene. The 1977 Great Britain touring team to Australia and New Zealand line-up as follows: back row (left to right): S. Wright, L. Dyl, T. Martyn, P. Hogan, D. Ward, W. Francis. middle row: S. Lloyd, A. Hodkinson, E. Bowman, J. Mills,

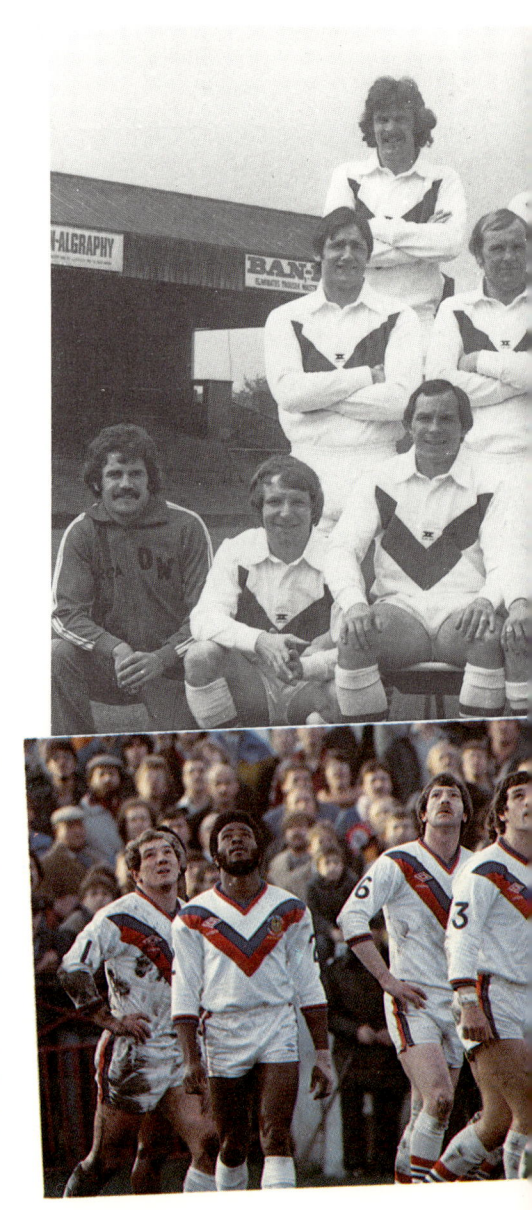

G. Nicholls, E. Cunningham, J. Holmes. front row: D. Watkins (coach), K. Gill, K. Fielding,. G. Fairburn, R. Parker (Manager), R. Millward (Capt.), K. Elwell, S. Nash, L. Casey, D. Wright (physiotherapist).

Spot the ball: members of the 1983 Great Britain team seem to be looking for inspiration against France.

Cups and competitions/5

proportion (about one-third) is ploughed into the game to help clubs to develop. A Rugby League Capital Development Fund has been set up to give grants and loans to clubs to help improve facilities where it matters — building stands and dressing-rooms, constructing new drainage systems, improving floodlighting.

Howes believes that, while sponsorship money is tempting and such money is well worth seeking, sponsors can disappear as quickly as they come, depending as they do on the economic climate and the shifting marketing policies of companies. So he prefers to regard sponsorship money as a welcome bonus, and no more than that. It is the paying spectator who keeps rugby league clubs in business, and any money that is earned outside that should be treated separately. Hence a proportion of the extra cash sponsorship brings in is put into long-term investments that the clubs could not otherwise afford.

With the State Express Challenge Cup, almost one-third of the £110,000 sponsorship goes into improving the game at club level. This policy meets with the full approval of the sponsors, who are happy to see the game develop under their patronage. Prizes are a bonus for the players rather than part of their wages.

The amount of money that the television companies pay for the privilege of showing league and cup matches is a closely-guarded secret, but is understood to be considerably less than they have been asked to find to cover association football matches. Some years ago, there was a special competition called the BBC-2 floodlit trophy, games of which the second half only would be transmitted live, usually on a Tuesday night. It was begun in 1965, and it was open to professional clubs with permanent floodlights, who played mid-week games in the first half of the season.

Towards the end of the competition's 13-season run, the BBC switched from live coverage to edited highlights screened later in the evening, which increased the audiences substantially at the games and in front of television sets. Financial cutbacks at the BBC meant the end of the competition after the 1979–80 season, despite prize money of £30,000 that year. Herein lies the moral: when the sponsor withdrew, the competition died with it and there is now no 'floodlit' competition as such.

If all the competitions in rugby league relied solely on sponsors for their existence, some would not exist at all now. Nevertheless, the 13-year run of the BBC-2 floodlit trophy did have one compensation: it brought poorly-supported Bramley the only trophy in the club's 96-year history. Ironically, however, that 'floodlit' final in 1973 had to be played in daylight because of the threat of a power strike.

To be fair to the BBC, covering floodlit matches is not easy, for only a handful of league grounds in Britain have night lights powerful enough for television cameras to get a clear view of play. Putting up the ancillary lighting needed can cost the television companies £10,000 or more per game, and so it is no surprise that their coverage of the evening games is not as extensive as it could be.

Right
Andy Gregory, of Widnes, is encircled by Hull players in the 1983 premiership final; and Fulham are obviously delighted at winning the second division title.

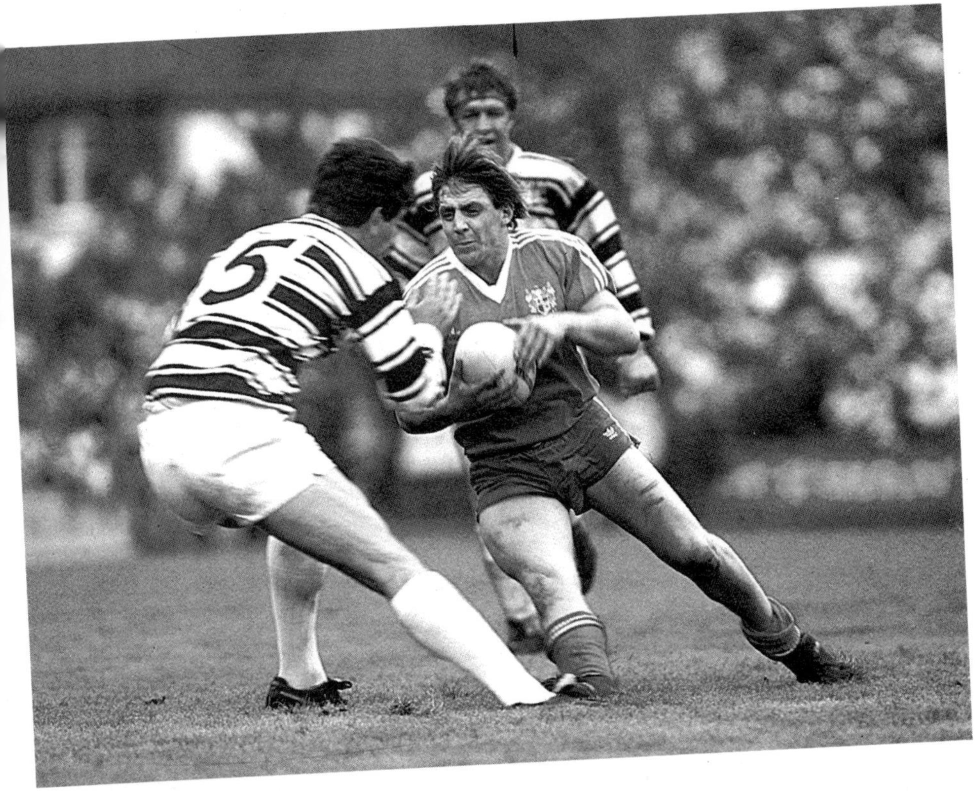

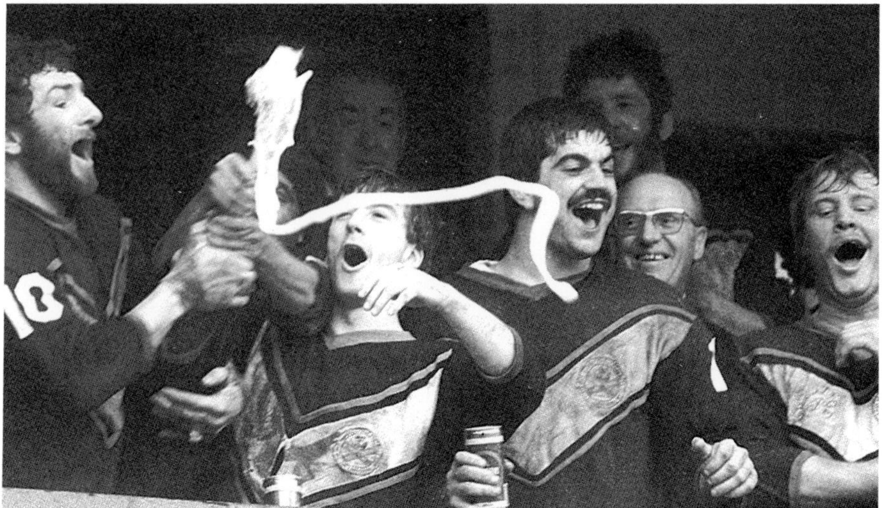

Equipment

Critics of rugby league often say that the players cannot be as tough as they are in other sports because they wear padding. Only in this way, it is said, can they withstand the knocks and tumbles in the same way as American grid-iron footballers do. Other sports are tougher because players have less protection from injury, they say.

Nothing could be further from the truth. More than half of the rugby league players who take the field each Sunday wear no additional padding at all. Moreover, anyone who has been in a dressing-room after a game knows how little protection padding affords.

League is a tough game, and although the laws do permit players to wear a certain degree of padding (provided it is not rigid, and so does not endanger other players), most players find padding too restrictive. The principal kit consists of distinctive jerseys, shorts and socks, and boots. In the event of a clash of colours between two sides, then the away side may be asked to wear a different strip (as in association football, but not in rugby union, where the home team changes).

The laws state specifically that a player shall not wear anything that might prove dangerous to other players, and nowhere is this more important than the studs on the boots. Although rugby league does not involve any rucks or mauls, the old-fashioned pile-ups, a player who is tackled can receive grievous injuries if another player falls on him while he is on the ground and the studs come into contact with him. Hence studs must be of the type that can cause no more injury than a nasty bruise. The only specific detail is that studs must, by the laws of the game, 'be no less than 8 mm in diameter at the apex and, if made of metal, shall have rounded edges.'

Referees are encouraged by the

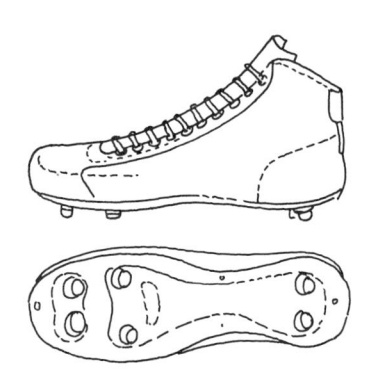

Boots and studs: players must not wear any clothing which might be dangerous. The minimum diameter of a stud is 8mm and the edge of the stud has to be rounded if it is made of metal.

Rugby League to inspect players' equipment before the start of the game to make sure that the start or progress of the game is not held up when the referee sees a player wearing illegal objects. Even so it is the player's responsibility to make sure he wears nothing that would contravene the laws of the game, such as rings or necklaces that could injure an opponent, or, indeed, insufficiently broad studs. Rugby league clubs wear distinctive jerseys for good reason. Colours of jerseys must be easily distinguishable if the referee is to keep proper control on the game.

On some grounds and in some weathers, similarity of strip can lead to confusion once shirts get muddy. So league teams go in for broad chevrons on the jerseys, or wide bands across the chest — on a muddy pitch, even white and black jerseys can be confused. In other sports, such differen-

League is tough: Charlie Stone, the Hull prop, leaves the Wembley pitch dripping in blood during the 1983 cup final (top). Fists fly in the international between Great Britain and France. Such outbursts are rarer in league than rugby union.

Equipment/2

tials do not seem to matter so much, either because players do not spend so much of the game pinned to the ground — in league, top players will make more than 40 tackles in an 80-minute match — or because it does not seem to matter so much. In league, the system is designed to help players, referees and spectators alike.

How tough are the players?

Arguments will always rage over how tough and how skilful rugby league players are compared with those in other sports, particularly rugby union. There is no doubt that many are extremely fit and, judging by the cuts and bruises they suffer in the course of the typical game, they must be tough, too.

Of course, comparisons are rarely put to the test. On only a few occasions have teams from rugby league and rugby union met, and then under extreme conditions. Two sides of servicemen — one representing the union game and the other the league — did play during the Second World War under 15-a-side union rules, a match which the league men won convincingly, though how good a test that was no-one can say. Superstars competitions organised for television audiences also provide a misleading guide: how can one compare the success of Des Drummond and Keith Fielding with that of Andy Ripley or Andy Irvine?

Nevertheless, rugby league is a tough game for the player, and it requires more skill than most people give it credit for. For Drummond, for example, to be able to run 100 metres in record time might not be that remarkable; for him to be able to avoid a tackle from two hefty opponents and to do so countless times in the course of a match for Leigh requires skill, stamina and endurance.

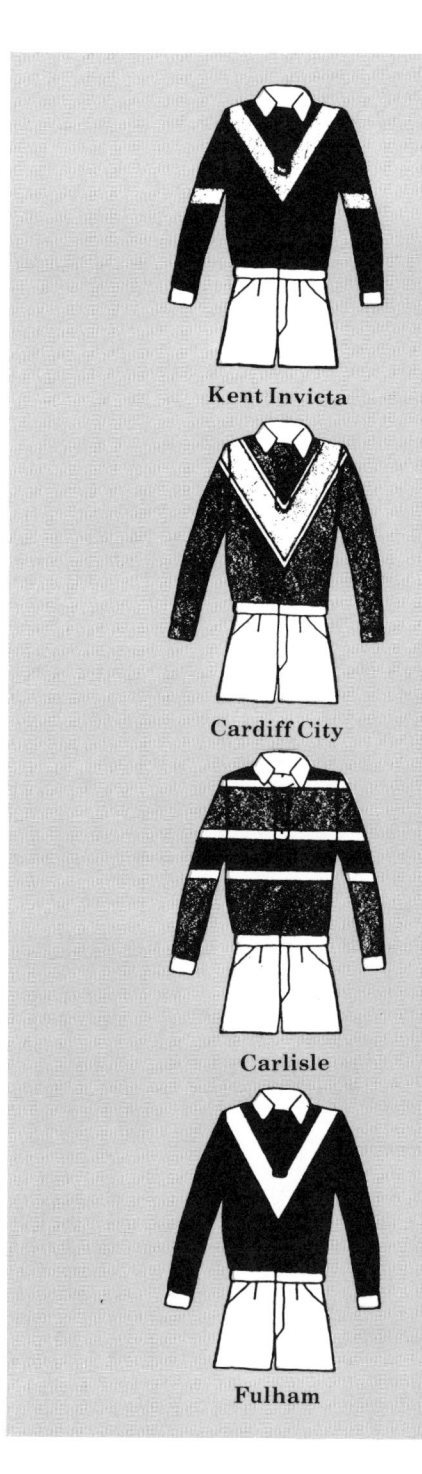

Kent Invicta

Cardiff City

Carlisle

Fulham

Nicknames

Rugby League clubs all acquire nicknames, although some do seem a trifle contrived. However, such titles are a Godsend to television commentators in particular, notably when Leeds play Leigh or Hull play Hull KR. Here are the most commonly-used nicknames for the sides in the league.

club	ground	nickname
Barrow	Craven Park	Shipbuilders
Batley	Mount Pleasant	Gallant Youths
Blackpool Borough	Borough Park	Milers ('Golden Mile')
Bradford Northern	Odsal Stadium	Northern
Bramley	McLaren Field	Villagers
Cardiff City	Ninian Park	Blue Dragons
Carlisle	Brunton Park	— (entered league 1981–2)
Castleford	Wheldon Road	Glassblowers
Dewsbury	Crown Flatt	— (none commonly used)
Doncaster	Tattersfield	Dons
Featherstone Rovers	Post Office Road	Colliers
Fulham	Craven Cottage	Londoners or Cottagers
Halifax	Thrum Hall	Thrum Hallers
Huddersfield	Fartown	— (none commonly used)
Hull	The Boulevard	Airlie Birds
Hull Kingston Rovers	Craven Park	Robins
Hunslet	Elland Road	— (none commonly used)
Huyton	Alt Park	— (none commonly used)
Keighley	Lawkholm Lane	Lawkholmers
Leeds	Headingley	Loiners
Leigh	Hilton Park	— (none commonly used)
Oldham	Watersheddings	Roughyeds
Rochdale Hornets	Athletic Ground	Hornets
St Helens	Knowsley Road	Saints
Salford	The Willows	Red Devils
Swinton	Station Road	Lions
Wakefield Trinity	Belle View	Dreadnoughts or Trinity
Warrington	Wilderspool	Wires (wire-making)
Whitehaven	Recreation Ground	Haven
Widnes	Naughton Park	Chemics (chemicals)
Wigan	Central Park	Riversiders
Workington Town	Derwent Park	Town
York	Wiggington Road	Wasps (jersey design)
Kent Invicta	Maidstone	— (entered 1983–4)

51

Team strips

All the club colours, with the league's newest additions on the previous page. Kent Invicta – black jersey, broad gold V, gold bands on arms. Cardiff – blue jerseys, yellow V with white piping. Carlisle – blue jerseys, broad red hoops with white piping. Fulham – black jerseys, white V with red piping.

Barrow

Batley

Dewsbury

Doncaster

Featherstone Rovers

Halifax

Huyton

Keighley

Leeds

Leigh

Swinton

Wakefield Trinity

Warrington

Whitehaven

Blackpool Borough	Bradford Northern	Bramley	Castleford
Huddersfield	Hull	Hull Kingston Rovers	Hunslet
Oldham	Rochdale Hornets	St Helens	Salford
Widnes	Wigan	Workington Town	York

Venues

Most rugby league grounds in Britain are situated close to centres of population, squeezed between rows of terrace houses, and most are in the industrial north. Small wonder that they seem uninspiring places to the viewer.

Stands tend to be old-fashioned and changing-room facilities are occasionally primitive. Only the boardroom and sometimes the bars are up-to-scratch. That is because rugby league grew out of the successful rugby union clubs of almost a century ago, and there has been a notable lack of investment since. In recent times, some grounds have been vastly improved — partly as a result of the Capital Development Fund and partly because of the realisation that a modern game needs modern facilities if it is to overcome the effect of the slump on attendances.

At some grounds, stands are starting to look badly in need of repair, drainage leaves much to be desired, the playing surface becomes impossibly muddy in winter, and facilities for television equipment and broadcasting are sadly lacking.

The television viewer can be duped into believing that conditions are perfect when really they are far from it. The ball that looks dry and clean may be like wet tripe; the kicker aiming at goal may be struggling not to twist his ankle on a rut as he runs up; the backs who are trying to pass the ball from one side of the field to the other may not be able to handle it quite as proficiently as they would at Twickenham simply because they are struggling to keep their balance on the slippery surface.

Another feature that never seems obvious on television is the slope. At

Craven Cottage: the players take the field and the scoreboard records a try.

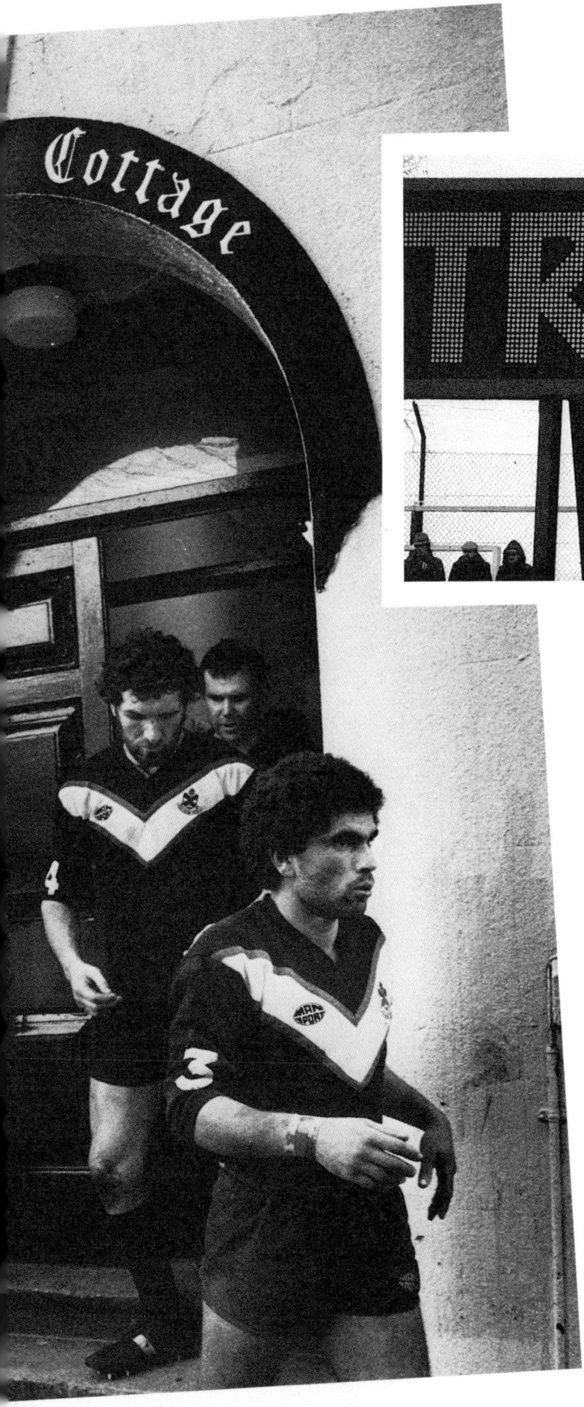
Cottage

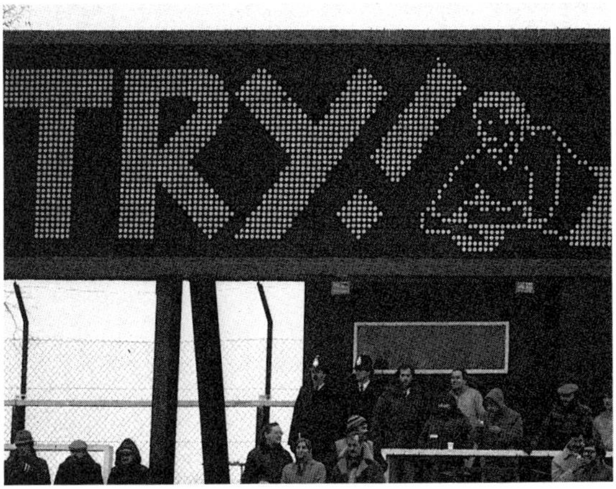
TRY!

Venues/2

the ironically-named Crown Flatt, home of Dewsbury RL club, the slope to one corner is so severe that players pray that they can run up it in the first half and down it in the second (when they are tired).

Rugby league clubs have a habit of calling their grounds names that almost poke fun at themselves. Mount Pleasant, home of Batley, is the wildest, most cheerless venue it is possible to find, saved only by the warmth of the club's hospitality. The Boulevard, home of Hull, is no Hollywood, either.

The average accommodation at rugby league grounds seems to be improving steadily. Some of the clubs spent money on improvements and the entry of several new clubs that share grounds with soccer sides such as Cardiff City (Ninian Park) and Fulham (Craven Cottage) has helped raise the standard. Each have good television-quality floodlighting and ample room for spectators and players alike.

What makes the difference is that football clubs are geared to large crowds and have room for keeping spectators and players apart. Their pitches are also, by tradition, level, well-screened and have full-time ground staff who keep the grass in good condition.

Joining forces with a soccer club also means that new clubs are not as pressed for cash to pay rates and general upkeep as the new club playing rugby league only would be. So a crowd of 3,000 at, say, Ninian Park would mean that the club would at least break even on the day, especially as rugby league supporters spend on average twice as much as football fans once they get through the turnstiles — and, more to the point, they cause much less damage and require far less policing.

Dewsbury's ironically named Crown Flatt ground which has an infamous slope.

Venues/3

Wembley

By far the most effective public relations arrangement ever made by any sport was the deal that took the Challenge Cup final to Wembley. Some 95,000 can be accommodated for the final at the Empire Stadium, only 2,000 fewer than the soccer final, which is also held usually in May.

The league limits the numbers at the Wembley final — albeit only by 2,000 — because the game is watched largely by families, who want a little more shoulder room than hordes of football supporters do.

The decision to go to London with the primary knock-out final was taken in 1928, when travelling was not as easy as it is today. But so popular has the Wembley trip become for league supporters that plays, books and films have been produced to record, fictionally, the weekend away from home.

Yet the record attendance at a rugby league match does not belong to Wembley stadium. It belongs to Odsal stadium, home of Bradford Northern, where 102,569 people saw Warrington play Halifax in the 1954 Challenge Cup final replay.

The first Wembley final, in 1929, drew a crowd of 41,500, and the capacity has been reached in 1966, 1970 and 1978. It has become such a familiar part of the rugby league year that it seems unlikely that the final will ever be staged in the North, other than for a replay, again.

Changing faces: top, Hull KR fans with their red scarves and favours support their side at Wembley in 1981; and Hull followers in cheerful mood outside the famous ground before suffering the agonies of defeat in 1983. Bottom, the wildness of Batley's home ground, Mount Pleasant.

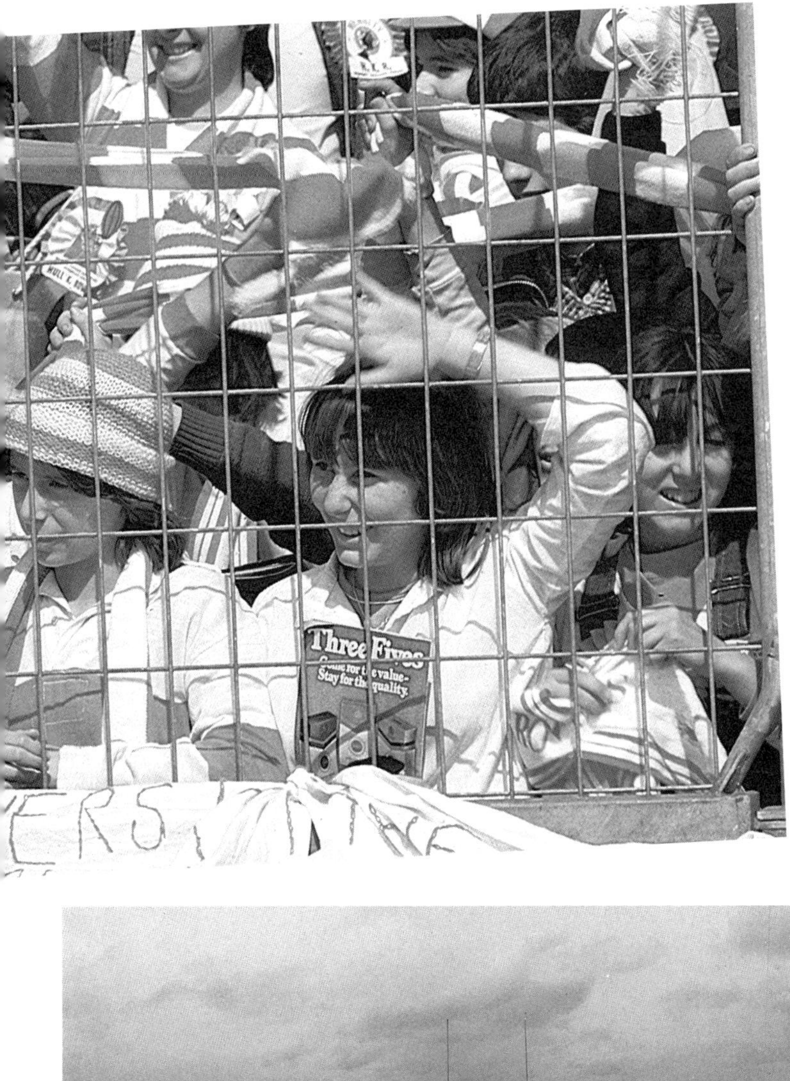
Three Fives
Stay for the quality.

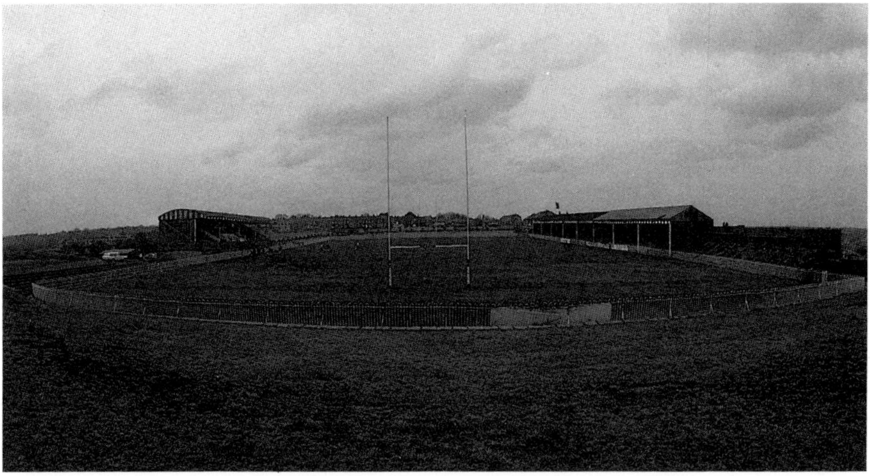

People in the media

There is no doubt that rugby league's efforts to become a respected national sport has suffered through the way it has been presented on television. Successive commentators and producers have, understandably, presented it as a colourful spectacle, a regional game with strong entertainment value, homely characters and a working-class penchant for beer and meat pies. Though these characteristics exist throughout the league, the television people have tended to forget that the game is as honourable a sport as any other.

So the cloth cap, Comic Cuts image of rugby league has been preserved long after it should have disappeared. The game has a fascination in itself: anyone who has witnessed more than a handful of 'live' games knows that it is compulsive viewing; those who watch it only on television sometimes see it only as a piece of showmanship. Many people in the media have tried to put that right. Keith Macklin, *The Times* rugby league correspondent and broadcaster has helped broaden the public's understanding of the game. So, too has Bill Fallowfield, one-time secretary of the Rugby League itself.

Macklin is involved in ITV's magazine programme *RL action*. It is shown on Monday evenings on Granada, Yorkshire and Border TV.

The name most readily associated with television commentary is Eddie Waring, whose reputation as a personality lives on long after he himself gave up live commentary at games. Waring's great contribution was to popularise what was seen thirty years ago as one of those games only northerners understood. He brought the game into areas it had never reached before, and he became a folk-hero, much impersonated by comedians — the greatest tribute of all. However, one of the penalties was that Waring became better known for his catch-phrases, such as 'early bath,' and 'up-and-under'; it endeared him to the public, but it deflected their attention from the game they were supposed to be watching.

You can still see signs of the Waring legacy in present television presentation. Though Alex Murphy and Ray French, the two commentators who looked after BBC's presentation of the game in the 1982–3 season, tried hard to foster greater understanding of the game, even they resorted to dry wit in a bid to make the game more attractive to the public. They evolved phrases like 'British Beef' to add colour to a game that hardly needs it.

The man who writes the captions when a player is being spotlighted even got into the act once, when a hound wandered on to the pitch and refused to leave, the caption writer put the name 'R. Dog' on the screen. Very funny, but not something that would be done at Twickenham or Hampden Park, surely.

So it is a moot point in the Rugby League as to whether taking a light-hearted view of the game is doing more for the reputation of the sport nationally than the straight-laced Bill McLaren-type commentary, with its emphasis on biographical detail and information. As long as there is humour on and off the field, family attendance, and the desire of television to entertain at all costs, the game will never be taken completely seriously. However, those who are now responsible for television presentation of the game are acutely conscious of the criticisms levelled at them by the 'purists' who yearn for the game to be taken on its own merits, as both football and rugby union are now.

Eddie Waring on retirement. Here he is with Ernest Kirkwood, the Lord Mayor of Hull, and the latter's wife.

Alex Murphy

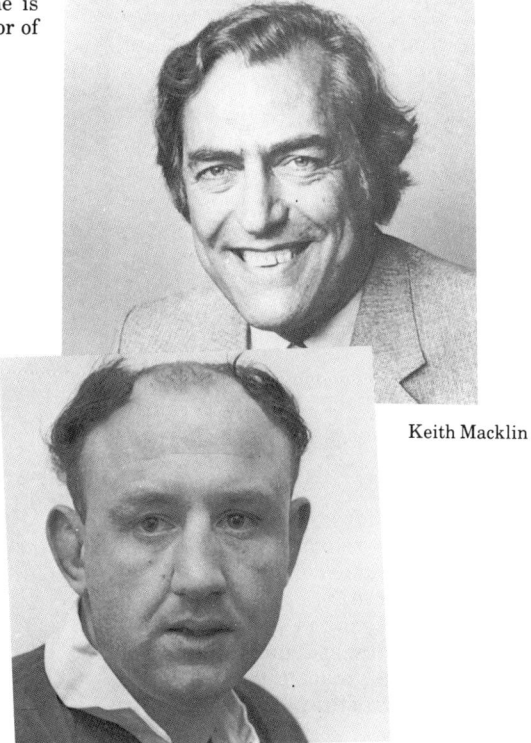

Keith Macklin

Ray French

Statistics

Rugby league supporters everywhere love statistics, many of which are updated weekly by headquarters in Leeds. Although most other sports rely on clubs to keep a record of their achievements, the notable exception being athletics, rugby league officials have a long tradition of keeping tabs on the game, and make sure they get the information they need from statistics supplied by clubs at the end of each home match. Here are just a few to whet your appetite:

Highest score: Huddersfield 119–2 v Swinton Park, 28 February 1914.

Longest unbeaten run: Huddersfield, 37 wins and 3 draws, 1914–5.

Most points in a match: George West (Hull Kingston Rovers), 11 tries and 10 goals (53 points) v Brookland Rovers in a Challenge cup match, March 1905.

Most points in a career: Neil Fox, 6,220. He played 19 seasons, with Wakefield Trinity between 1956 and 1979, also appearing for Bradford Northern, Hull KR, York, Bramley and Huddersfield, not to mention many representative matches.

Most goals in a match: Jim Sullivan, 22 in a Challenge cup game v Flimby and Fothergill, 1925.

Most tries in a season: Albert Rosenfield (Huddersfield), 80 in 1913–4.

Most points in a season: Lewis Jones (Leeds), 496 in 1956–7.

Most tries in a career: Brian Bevan (Warrington) 796, 1946–1964 (740 of them for Warrington).

Most goals in a season: David Watkins (Salford) 221. Watkins also holds the record for the longest unbroken sequence of matches (92) in which he both played and scored. His run brought Salford 929 points between August 1972 and April 1974.

Longest winning league run: 31 matches, Wigan (the last eight matches of 1969–70 and the first 23 of 1970–1). Only Hull, who won all of their 26 division two matches in 1978–9, have gone through a league season without defeat.

Longest losing league run: 40 matches, Doncaster (division two November 1975–April 1977. In 1906–7, Liverpool City lost all their league matches, the only time a team playing more than 12 league matches has not won one. Not surprisingly, the club disbanded after that one season. One of their matches, against Bramley, was a draw.

Results
Challenge Cup

Year	Team	Score	Opponent	Score	Attendance
1960	Wakefield Trinity	38	Hull	5	79,773
1961	St Helens	12	Wigan	6	94,672
1962	Wakefield Trinity	12	Huddersfield	6	81,263
1963	Wakefield Trinity	25	Wigan	10	84,492
1964	Widnes	13	Hull Kingston Rovers	5	84,488
1965	Wigan	20	Hunslet	16	89,016
1966	St Helens	21	Wigan	2	*98,536
1967	Featherstone Rovers	17	Barrow	12	76,290
1968	Leeds	11	Wakefield Trinity	10	87,100
1969	Castleford	11	Salford	6	*97,939
1970	Castleford	7	Wigan	2	95,255
1971	Leigh	24	Leeds	7	85,514
1972	St Helens	16	Leeds	13	89,495
1973	Featherstone Rovers	33	Bradford Northern	14	72,395
1974	Warrington	24	Featherstone Rovers	9	77,400

1975	Widnes	14	Warrington	7	85,098
1976	St Helens	20	Widnes	5	89,982
1977	Leeds	16	Widnes	7	80,871
1978	Leeds	14	St Helens	12	*96,000
1979	Widnes	12	Wakefield Trinity	3	94,218
1980	Hull Kingston Rovers	10	Hull	5	*95,000
1981	Widnes	18	Hull Kingston Rovers	9	92,496
1982	Hull	14	Widnes	14	92,147
	Hull (at Elland Road, Leeds)	18	Widnes	9	41,171
1983	Featherstone Rovers	14	Hull	12	84,745

* capacity attendance

Most wins: Leeds, 10
Most finals: Wigan, 15
Highest score in final: 1960

Lance Todd trophy

1960	Tommy Harris (Hull)
1961	Dick Huddart (St Helens)
1962	Neil Fox (Wakefield Trinity)
1963	Harold Poynton (Wakefield Trinity)
1964	Frank Collier (Widnes)
1965	Ray Ashby (Wigan)
	Brian Gabbitas (Hunslet)
1966	Len Killeen (St Helens)
1967	Carl Dooler (Featherstone Rovers)
1968	Don Fox (Wakefield Trinity)
1969	Malcolm Reilly (Castleford)
1970	Bill Kirkbride (Castleford)
1971	Alex Murphy (Leigh)
1972	Kel Coslett (St Helens)
1973	Steve Nash (Featherstone Rovers)
1974	Derek Whitehead (Warrington)
1975	Ray Dutton (Widnes)
1976	Geoff Pimblett (St Helens)
1977	Steve Pitchford (Leeds)
1978	George Nicholls (St Helens)
1979	David Topliss (Wakefield Trinity)
1980	Brian Lockwood (Hull Kingston Rovers)
1981	Mick Burke (Widnes)
1982	Eddie Cunningham (Widnes)
1983	David Hobbs (Featherstone Rovers)

John Player trophy

1971–72	Halifax	22	Wakefield Trinity	11	(at Bradford)
1972–73	Leeds	12	Salford	7	(at Huddersfield)
1973–74	Warrington	27	Rochdale Hornets	16	(at Wigan)
1974–75	Bradford Northern	3	Widnes	2	(at Warrington)
1975–76	Widnes	19	Hull	13	(at Leeds)
1976–77	Castleford	25	Blackpool Borough	15	(at Salford)
1977–78	Warrington	9	Widnes	4	(at St Helens)
1978–79	Widnes	16	Warrington	4	(at St Helens)
1979–80	Bradford Northern	6	Widnes	0	(at Leeds)
1980–81	Warrington	12	Barrow	5	(at Wigan)
1981–82	Hull	12	Hull Kingston Rovers	4	(at Leeds)
1982–83	Wigan	15	Leeds	4	(at Leeds)

Statistics/2

Premiership final

1975	Leeds	26	St Helens	11	(at Wigan)
1976	St Helens	15	Salford	2	(at Swinton)
1977	St Helens	32	Warrington	20	(at Swinton)
1978	Bradford Northern	17	Widnes	8	(at Swinton)
1979	Leeds	24	Bradford Northern	2	(at Huddersfield)
1980	Widnes	19	Bradford Northern	5	(at Swinton)
1981	Hull Kingston Rovers	11	Hull	7	(at Leeds)
1982	Widnes	23	Hull	8	(at Leeds)
1983	Widnes	22	Hull	10	(at Leeds)

League leaders

1973–74	Salford
1974–75	St Helens
1975–76	Salford
1976–77	Featherstone Rovers
1977–78	Widnes
1978–79	Hull Kingston Rovers
1979–80	Bradford Northern
1980–81	Bradford Northern
1981–82	Leigh
1982–83	Hull

Bibliography

The following books are recommended as sources of further information on rugby league:

Encyclopaedia of Rugby League Football, Julian Huxley and David Howes, published by Robert Hale (London).

David Watkins, an autobiography, By David Watkins, published by Cassell Ltd (London).

History of Rugby League Football, Keith Macklin (Stanley Paul).

Rothmans Rugby League Yearbook, David Howes and Raymond Fletcher, published by Rothmans Publications Ltd, (Aylesbury, Bucks.).

Know the game: Rugby League (official illustrated handbook of the Rugby League), published by EP Publishing (Wakefield).

All of the above can be ordered from the Rugby League, RL Headquarters, Chapeltown Road, Leeds 7.

Acknowledgements

In the preparation of this book, we are most grateful to David Howes, of the Rugby League; Keith Macklin and to Mr J. A. Saville, of Hull, who has kindly made available historic photographs from his priceless collections. Photographs of Lee Crooks, Des Drummond, David Hobbs, Roger Millward (with trophy) and Steve Quinn by Andrew Varley; Rugby School by Mary Evans Picture Library.

The life of Benjamin Barker, a notorious highwayman, from his youth to his death; who was executed at Chelmsford on Friday the 18th of May, 1750, Containing a full account of his wicked behaviour.

The life of Benjamin Barker, a notorious highwayman, from his youth to his death; who was executed at Chelmsford on Friday the 18th of May, 1750, ... Containing a full account of his wicked behaviour ... together with the many robberies he and his gang co
Multiple Contributors, See Notes
ESTCID: T073619
Reproduction from British Library
With a half-title.
London : printed for J. Underwood, and sold at Aldersgate, the Royal-Exchange, and by most booksellers in town and country; likewise by the hawkers who carry the news, 1750.
[4],16p. ; 8°

ECCO
Eighteenth Century
Collections Online
Print Editions

Gale ECCO Print Editions

Relive history with *Eighteenth Century Collections Online*, now available in print for the independent historian and collector. This series includes the most significant English-language and foreign-language works printed in Great Britain during the eighteenth century, and is organized in seven different subject areas including literature and language; medicine, science, and technology; and religion and philosophy. The collection also includes thousands of important works from the Americas.

The eighteenth century has been called "The Age of Enlightenment." It was a period of rapid advance in print culture and publishing, in world exploration, and in the rapid growth of science and technology – all of which had a profound impact on the political and cultural landscape. At the end of the century the American Revolution, French Revolution and Industrial Revolution, perhaps three of the most significant events in modern history, set in motion developments that eventually dominated world political, economic, and social life.

In a groundbreaking effort, Gale initiated a revolution of its own: digitization of epic proportions to preserve these invaluable works in the largest online archive of its kind. Contributions from major world libraries constitute over 175,000 original printed works. Scanned images of the actual pages, rather than transcriptions, recreate the works *as they first appeared.*

Now for the first time, these high-quality digital scans of original works are available via print-on-demand, making them readily accessible to libraries, students, independent scholars, and readers of all ages.

For our initial release we have created seven robust collections to form one the world's most comprehensive catalogs of 18th century works.

Initial Gale ECCO Print Editions collections include:

> ### *History and Geography*
> Rich in titles on English life and social history, this collection spans the world as it was known to eighteenth-century historians and explorers. Titles include a wealth of travel accounts and diaries, histories of nations from throughout the world, and maps and charts of a world that was still being discovered. Students of the War of American Independence will find fascinating accounts from the British side of conflict.

Social Science
Delve into what it was like to live during the eighteenth century by reading the first-hand accounts of everyday people, including city dwellers and farmers, businessmen and bankers, artisans and merchants, artists and their patrons, politicians and their constituents. Original texts make the American, French, and Industrial revolutions vividly contemporary.

Medicine, Science and Technology
Medical theory and practice of the 1700s developed rapidly, as is evidenced by the extensive collection, which includes descriptions of diseases, their conditions, and treatments. Books on science and technology, agriculture, military technology, natural philosophy, even cookbooks, are all contained here.

Literature and Language
Western literary study flows out of eighteenth-century works by Alexander Pope, Daniel Defoe, Henry Fielding, Frances Burney, Denis Diderot, Johann Gottfried Herder, Johann Wolfgang von Goethe, and others. Experience the birth of the modern novel, or compare the development of language using dictionaries and grammar discourses.

Religion and Philosophy
The Age of Enlightenment profoundly enriched religious and philosophical understanding and continues to influence present-day thinking. Works collected here include masterpieces by David Hume, Immanuel Kant, and Jean-Jacques Rousseau, as well as religious sermons and moral debates on the issues of the day, such as the slave trade. The Age of Reason saw conflict between Protestantism and Catholicism transformed into one between faith and logic -- a debate that continues in the twenty-first century.

Law and Reference
This collection reveals the history of English common law and Empire law in a vastly changing world of British expansion. Dominating the legal field is the *Commentaries of the Law of England* by Sir William Blackstone, which first appeared in 1765. Reference works such as almanacs and catalogues continue to educate us by revealing the day-to-day workings of society.

Fine Arts
The eighteenth-century fascination with Greek and Roman antiquity followed the systematic excavation of the ruins at Pompeii and Herculaneum in southern Italy; and after 1750 a neoclassical style dominated all artistic fields. The titles here trace developments in mostly English-language works on painting, sculpture, architecture, music, theater, and other disciplines. Instructional works on musical instruments, catalogs of art objects, comic operas, and more are also included.

The BiblioLife Network

This project was made possible in part by the BiblioLife Network (BLN), a project aimed at addressing some of the huge challenges facing book preservationists around the world. The BLN includes libraries, library networks, archives, subject matter experts, online communities and library service providers. We believe every book ever published should be available as a high-quality print reproduction; printed on-demand anywhere in the world. This insures the ongoing accessibility of the content and helps generate sustainable revenue for the libraries and organizations that work to preserve these important materials.

The following book is in the "public domain" and represents an authentic reproduction of the text as printed by the original publisher. While we have attempted to accurately maintain the integrity of the original work, there are sometimes problems with the original work or the micro-film from which the books were digitized. This can result in minor errors in reproduction. Possible imperfections include missing and blurred pages, poor pictures, markings and other reproduction issues beyond our control. Because this work is culturally important, we have made it available as part of our commitment to protecting, preserving, and promoting the world's literature.

GUIDE TO FOLD-OUTS MAPS and OVERSIZED IMAGES

The book you are reading was digitized from microfilm captured over the past thirty to forty years. Years after the creation of the original microfilm, the book was converted to digital files and made available in an online database.

In an online database, page images do not need to conform to the size restrictions found in a printed book. When converting these images back into a printed bound book, the page sizes are standardized in ways that maintain the detail of the original. For large images, such as fold-out maps, the original page image is split into two or more pages

Guidelines used to determine how to split the page image follows:

• Some images are split vertically; large images require vertical and horizontal splits.
• For horizontal splits, the content is split left to right.
• For vertical splits, the content is split from top to bottom.
• For both vertical and horizontal splits, the image is processed from top left to bottom right.

THE
LIFE
OF
BENJAMIN BARKER,
A NOTORIOUS
HIGHWAYMAN, &c.

[*This Day is Publish'd, Price Four-pence,*]

THE Life of *Thomas Munn*, alias the *Gentleman Brickmaker*, alias *Tom the Smuggler*, who was executed with *John Hall*, alias *Rich*, on Friday the 6th of *April*, 1750, at *Chelmsford*, and hung in Chains near *Rumford* Gallows, for robbing the *Yarmouth* Mail on the 20th of *Jul.* last. Publish'd from the Copy all wrote with his own Hand, and delivered by him the Morning of his Execution to Mr *Thomas Venden*, Turnkey of his Majesty's Gaol at *Chelmsford* in *Essex*, with a particular Desire it might be printed. To which is added, a short Account of the Life of *John Hall*, his Accomplice, and the Manner of their being taken. Likewise their Behaviour at the Place of Execution.

London Printed for *Thomas Harris* at *Aldersgate*, C. *Corbet* in *Fleetstreet*, and sold by most Booksellers in Town and Country, and by the Hawkers who carry the News

THE
LIFE
OF
BENJAMIN BARKER,
A NOTORIOUS
HIGHWAYMAN,
FROM HIS
YOUTH to his DEATH;

WHO WAS

Executed at *Chelmsford* on *Friday* the 18th of *May*, 1750, for robbing Mr. JOHN BLOWER, of *Bocking*, in the *Bury* Coach.

CONTAINING

A Full Account of his wicked Behaviour from his Infancy, with the many Intrigues during his Apprenticeship with lewd Women, &c.

TOGETHER WITH

The many Robberies he and his Gang committed in divers Parts of *England*.

ALSO

An Account of his Trial, Behaviour in Gaol after Sentence, and dying Words at the Place of Execution

---

LONDON.

Printed for J UNDERWOOD, in *Fleet street*, and sold at *Aldersgate*, the *Royal-Exchange*, and by most Booksellers in Town and Country, likewise by the Hawkers who carry the News. 1750   (Price Three-pence.)

THE LIFE OF *BENJAMIN BARKER*,

A notorious Highwayman.

THIS *Benjamin Barker* was a Native of *Saffron-Walden* in *Essex*. He was born in the remarkable mad Year 1720, but as to the Day or Month of his Nativity he could not exactly determine. Tho' his Parents were in but indifferent Circumstances, yet they were honest as well as industrious; and as he was his Mother's Darling, there was no Money spared in Reason, that might contribute towards his future Happiness, by bestowing on him an Education, even beyond their Income. They put him therefore, whilst young, to a very considerable School, in the County of *Essex* abovementioned, where, being a Youth of sprightly Parts, he excelled most of his School-Fellows, of his tender Age, in those little Accomplishments

complishments which were recommended to his Practice by his indulgent Parents; insomuch that before he was eight Years of Age, he could read without the least Hesitation, write a legible Hand, and give a very satisfactory Account of the first four Rules in Arithmetic, to the great Joy of his Father and Mother, as well as to the Credit and Reputation of his Master.

Before he attained however the ninth Year of his Age, he began to be very untoward, disobedient to his Mother, and ungrateful both to her and his Master, who, as the one spared no Cost, so the other spared no Pains, in giving him the necessary Instructions for his early Improvement in the several Branches of Literature, which he found his tender Years capable of.

He would frequently, before he was ten Years old, purloin his Play-Fellow's Books, and clandestinely make them away, in Order to furnish his Pocket with petty Expences; and so from one little Act of Unluckiness to another, would proceed to Facts of a more criminal Nature; notwithstanding he had always Cunning and Artifice enough to get clear, when he was suspected, by fixing the Blame on some innocent Companion, who had not equal Assurance with himself.

In short, he played so many unlucky Pranks between the Age of ten and fourteen, in many of which he was openly convicted, and for which

which he was as openly punished and exposed to Shame in the public School.

But his Master, finding that none of his friendly Admonitions, nor the severest of his Chastisements had the desired Effect upon him, or worked the least Reformation, he sent him home to his Parents with all the Testimonies of Contempt, and desired them to undertake the Task he was obliged to decline; and that for his Part, he would not admit of so bad an Example, to be shewn in his School, on any Account, notwithstanding he had no Objection to the Encouragement they gave him for the Improvement of their Son, which he always readily acknowledged was rather greater than less than their mean Circumstances could well admit of.

His Parents, being very honest and very indulgent, as we hinted before, received this unwelcome Message from his Master with Tears in their Eyes, but with Thanks however, for his Endeavours to reclaim this their naughty Son.

From the Time he left his School to the Time he was full fourteen Years of Age, they undertook the Drudgery of tutoring him themselves, but finding that neither fair Promises, severe Menaces, nor actual corporal Punishment, would deter him from the Commission of such evil Actions as they were perfectly ashamed of, they resolved to raise a small Sum of Money, in order to induce the first honest Tradesman

Tradesman that they could find to take him Apprentice.

Accordingly by that Time he had attained the fourteenth Year of his Age, they prevailed on a very industrious honest Blacksmith, in a Town far distant from the Place wherein they themselves resided, and one who knew nothing of his innate bad Qualities, to take him under his Tuition, and before he had Time to find out any of his enormous Pranks, through the Temptation of a few Guineas, bound him directly to his Service, by Indentures of Apprenticeship regularly signed and sealed, for the Term of seven Years.

Our young artful Apprentice, in some measure, approved of his new Settlement, and perceiving his Master a good natur'd Man, and his Mistress kinder to him than he could reasonably expect, he behaved for near the three first Years of his Servitude so well, that his Parents were over-joyed at his happy Situation, and the just Grounds they had, to hope he would prove a very faithful Servant to his Master, and a great Comfort to themselves, in their old Age.

The Scene, however, too soon changed; and by that Time he had attained the seventeenth Year of his Age, the old Sparks of his former Fire began to revive; and the older he grew, the more vicious and wicked was his Deportment

The

The first Transgression, of which he was convicted, was an Elopement from the Meeting on the Lord's Day; and as his Mistress was a Speaker amongst the Quakers, and very remarkable for the Sanctity of her Manners, took him very severely to Task, before his Master, after their Return from the Conventicle. She told him in very warm Terms, that he was a naughty Youth; that she feared the Light was not in him, and that in Case he was once addicted to contemn the Service of the Lord on his Holy Day, both she and her house should soon become Sufferers through his profane Practices.

Tho' the good Man joined with his Dame in her pious Exhortations, yet he thought her Reproofs too warm for a first Elopement; and therefore he told him, that upon a suitable Humiliation he should find Forgiveness for this first Offence

This Storm, thus happily blown over, our young Apprentice proved doubly diligent for a whole month after, and gave them all the outward Tokens of sincere Contrition for his first Act of Disodedience.

He was now more in Favour than ever, both with his Master and Mistress, it was not long however, before he cast a luscious Eye on *Abigail* their Maid, and being hale and handsome, he soon got into her good Graces.

This Amour, 'tis true, had a good Effect
for

for some considerable Time; he absented himself from all Company, and it was with great Difficulty that he could be prevailed with to stay an Hour from Home.

This Conduct of his still enhanc'd his Value in the Eyes of his innocent Master and Mistress, and they imagined themselves very happy in a faithful Servant.

All is not Gold, however, that glitters, and our young Apprentice, as soon as conveniently he could, crept to Bed to his dearly beloved *Abigail*, and, in short, in the Process of a few Months, her Belly beginning to rise higher than he could wish it, and for fear of a Discovery in the Family, added to that of the Overseer of the Parish, he came to an absolute Resolution with himself, to make an Elopement at once, whilst all was quiet, and to leave his Mistress in the Lurch, as well as his Place of Bondage, before he could be laid by the Heels for his Misdemeanors.

No sooner resolved on but done; the Plan was laid but on Saturday Night, and on the Lord's Day Morning, he moved off of the Premises, took with him all the Cloaths he had, as well as *Abigail's* Money, which he got from her, in their last amorous Adventure, and to'dly took his Flight for *Newmarket*; where he appeared in Masquerade, as an adept Jockey; his Exploits there, and his various shifting of the Scene from Place to Place, will be the subject Matter of the subsequent Pages.

No sooner were the Races over, where he made a considerable Figure, and by that Means presumed to lay several Wagers, without being suspected:

suspected: And as he happened to be very successful, he was caress'd by several of the Nobility; but more particularly by the Publicans, where he was lavish in his Expences, and paid as honourably for what he called for, if not more so, than any foreign Count, or Court Minister, that was resident there to partake of the Diversions of the Place.

Thus flushed with Success, and being, in the Opinion of most, some young country Heir to some old Miser, just happily arrived to an uninterrupted Possession of a very plentiful Estate, several Gamblers, Gamesters, and other humane Vultures, made their Court to him, in Hopes to fleece him, but as he soon opened his Case to them, and made them sensible he was as great an Impostor as themselves, he soon contracted an intimate Acquaintance with them; and they readily consented to make him Chairman of their Society.

As he was a Novice at the first Initiation, they let him into the Secret of shuffling and cutting the Cards, and dropping the Shilling, to draw in the unwary Countryman, or the Guinea, to make a Dupe of the unwary Country-Squire; and being a very apt Scholar, he took it all in, and in less than a Week's Time, he was as expert as the oldest Member of the Shuffling and Cutting Club.

Thus tutor'd, after living in the most profuse Manner, in Regard to drinking, whoring, and the other fashionable Vices of the Age, at *Newmarket*, for about three Weeks or a Month, it was agreed by the whole Assembly (Nem. Con) to break up their Court, and to remove to *London*.

As *Newmarket* was rather too far, for even the poorest of their Gang to foot it to *London*, they called a Court, and the principal Affair upon the Carpet turn'd upon the important Article of proper Vehicles, for the Conveyance of the respective Members of their Society to Covent-Garden; that is to say, to my *L—d M—ts*, the noted Receptacle for Gamblers and other Artificers in the Propagation of the sinking Fund. Whereupon it was unanimously agreed, for Expedition Sake, to steal as many Horses as were requisite for the Purpose. And as three fourths of them were honest Yorkshire-Men, a Committee of that County only, was appointed to furnish the whole Society with the best Saddle Naggs, that could be procured in the Place.

Accordingly a Parcel of Bridles, by Order of the Chairman, was purchased with ready Money; and as there were Nags enow grazing in the Fields adjacent to the Town, the whole Crew got up early one Morning, according to the Signal given, and each provided himself with a Horse for the proposed Expedition.

The Plot was so well laid, that notwithstanding a Hue-and-Cry was soon after them, they fled with too much Speed to be overtaken, and arrived safely at their wish'd-for Port.

They had not been long arrived at *Covent-Garden*, before our *Benjamin* got acquainted with one *S—ms*, a greater Adept in the Faculty of diving than any of the Gang he was now link'd with, in whose Conversation he he was particularly delighted; and with whom he contracted an intimate Friendship.

S——ms, being very gracious with several Ladies belonging to the Hundreds of *Drury,* and our *Benjamin,* tho' a true-born *Englishman,* being as promising a young Fellow, and as strong-back'd as most of the *Hibernian* Race, recommended him, as a Bully, fit for their Turn, in any Skirmish Abroad, as well as a Gallant capable of fighting with any one of them (by way of Pleasure and Frolick) between a Pair of Sheets as the stoutest B——n.

Our *Benjamin,* thus once well introduced, became a Favourite in a very short Time, and was soon planted in a snug Place, as Foreman to a Female Academy, where he play'd more Pranks, during his short Residence there in Indolence and Ease, than the most luscious Capuchin ever play'd in a Convent of Nuns.

That Sort of Life, however, not suiting his Inclination long (for he was naturally very sprightly and active) he sent his new favourite Companion S——ms a Summons to drink a Bowl of Punch at Mother *Midnight's,* at the Angel in *Drury-Lane,* on the *Sunday* following, as being an idle Day with them both, and accordingly S——ms very punctually met on the Day and the Hour proposed.

After a long and serious Debate, they jointly came to a Resolution, not to live like a Couple of worthless Drones, that are only Stallions to a Pack of Female Bees, as they had done for some Time past, but to act for the future like Men of Spirit and Intrepidity; to profess themselves Knights of the Sword, and Superintendants

intendants Extraordinary of his Majesty's Highways; and, for their own private Emolument, to patrole a-Nights as well as Days.

Preliminaries now settled, and the Oath of Secrecy (as is customary on the like Contracts) being warmly taken on both Sides, it was first agreed *(Nem. Con.)* to purchase two Pair of Pistols, for the more effectual Prosecution of the Plan laid down, and for their mutual Subsistence in a less servile Way than being the mock Heroes of a Bawdy-House.

In the second Place, it was agreed to make their first Excursion on the *Tuesday* following; and as S———ms was the more experienced Traveller, the Course they had to steer was wholly submitted to his superior Judgment. S—ms, therefore, proposed to his Comrade *Hounslow-Heath* for a proper Scene of Action, and as our *Benjamin* was wholly indifferent in that Particular, made no Objection to the Proposition.

On *Tuesday* Evening, accordingly, they set out about Dusk, and jogg'd on till they came to *Hounslow* Town, very cooly, from whence (after proper refreshment) they jogg'd on for *Stains*, and in their way met with a Physician and his Lady in their Coach, from whom they took a valuable Booty, which they divided to each others satisfaction at the *White Swan* at *Stains*, where they took up their Quarters, and behaved generously, and paid genteely.

Next morning they agreed to return again to *London*, but by another Road; and in their Way to visit *Hampton Court*.

Accordingly

Accordingly, early in the Morning, they took Horse, and pursued their Journey. Before they had got a mile on the Common leading to *Hampton*, who should overtake them but one of the Collectors of the County of *Surry*, whom they soon discover'd by his Discourse; and as they perceived his Baggs were swell'd with something more than a dirty Shirt, they determin'd to see the Inside of them, and immediately gave him the Word of Command to *Stand and Deliver*.

The Collector, presuming upon the mistaken Notion, *That One honest Man will frighten half a Score Thieves*, instantly prepared to stand in his own Defence, but his Courage proved very ill-timed S———ms, without farther Ceremony shot his Horse, and *Ben* with his Pistol cock'd, was ready to serve the Gentleman himself in the same manner had he made any further Resistance; but he thought it most prudent to submit to the Loss of his money, rather than to put his Life any more in Jeopardy upon such unequal Terms. Having stripp'd him of all he had, to the Amount of 100 l. they wish'd him a pleasant Walk, and then looking up at the Sun, took their Leave of him with this friendly Admonition· *Sure, Sir, the County we scorn to ruin a single Man, but there's no Harm, you know, in collecting a Trifle from the Public*.

No sooner was this sarcastical Advice given, but they set Spurs to their Horses, and made the best of their way to *London*, without staying at *Hampton*, having made pretty good use of their time during this short Excursion

The *Cole-Hole* in *Drury-lane* was their usual Rendezvous, and thither they arrived, and shared the Profits of their Plunder, and having indulged themselves a few Days in all the Gratifications of Debauchery and Lust, they at Length agreed to part in order to avoid a Discovery. *Ben* travell'd with the Remains of his Booty into *Suffolk* with a Resolution to live honest, and accordingly hired himself to a Farmer, having first equipp'd himself properly for that purpose. Here he got acquainted with one *Munns*, (lately executed at *Chelmsford* for robbing the *Yarmouth* Mail, and hung in Chains near *Rumford* Gallows) who took great Delight in his Company, and in a very little while they discover'd to each other the methods they formerly follow'd to get Money, and agreed to pursue them. they first began with Shuffling and Cutting the Cards to cheat the young Country Fellows, who little suspected them; this Practice succeeding, *Ben* soon quitted his Service, and betook himself wholly to his old Trade, in which being seconded by *Munns*, they committed a Series of Villanies hardly to be parallell'd, all which, together with their artful Escapes, being already publish'd, we shall refer our Readers to that Account, and proceed to the Adventures of *Ben*, after parting with *Munns*.

Ben travell'd from *Ipswich* to *Braintree*, and in his Way attack'd a Gentleman with the usual Ceremony, and robb'd him of his Watch and some Silver; the Gentleman desired he

* *See the Life of Munns wrote by himself, a Pamphlet worth perusing. Price 4d.*

would

would give him the Seal from his Watch, it belonging to his Family, which he accordingly gave him, and afterwards sold the Watch for two Guineas

The next Person he attack'd was *Martha Goodey*, near *Sudbury* in *Suffolk*, whom he robbed of her Apron and thirty Shillings in Silver on the King's Highway.

And, lastly, he attack'd the *Bury* Coach in the following manner; as the Coachman was driving from *Sudbury*, when he came to a Place called *Bannington-Hill* in *Essex*, a few Miles from *Sudbury*, *Barker* came full tilt up the Hill, and called to the Coachman to Stop, which he accordingly did, thinking he had got a Passenger, however *Ben* soon convinced him of the Mistake, came to the Coach Door, and, in the usual Manner, attack'd Mr *John Blower*, who was in the Coach alone, robbed him of a Sum of Money, and order'd the Coachman to drive on

He was taken in *Bannington* a few Days after, and committed to *Chelmsford* Goal by *Robert Tweed*, Esq, of *Halsted*, charged on the Oath of *John Blower*, and by his own Confession; and also on the Oath of *Martha Goodey*, and by his own Confession, with robbing them on the King's Highway as aforesaid

He was accordingly tried at the last Assizes at *Chelmsford*, and condemn'd to be hanged with *Evans* and *Hall*, but was afterwards respited from time to time, till at last the Warrant came down for his Execution, which was order'd on the 15th of *May*

The following is the Copy of an Advertisement relating to the Robbery, which has been inserted in the Ipswich Courant.

WHEREAS it has been reported by several Persons, that I BENJAMIN BARKER, now under Sentence of Death in his Majesty's Goal of CHELMSFORD in the County of ESSEX, for robbing Mr JOHN BLOWER of Bocking in the said County, on the King's Highway, have declared, That I took from the said John Blower only some Silver and Half-pence, I the said BENJAMIN BARKER do confess that such Reports are intirely false, and I do also declare, that at the Time I robbed him, being in great Confusion, and standing on a Side-Bank, my Feet slipped from the Place where I stood, and I verily believe the said John Blower lost the whole Sum of Money he said he did, at the Time I robbed him, and that I might drop it in the Hurry and Confusion I was in; I do also declare, that no Person was with me at the Time I robbed the said John Blower, and that what I said when I was before Mr Tweed of Halsted, relating to Smith and Pamenter being concerned with me in the Robbery, is intirely false; and I do beg Mr Tweed's Pardon for the same. I do also declare, that the printed Paper exposed to Sale last Friday, called my DYING SPEECH, is intirely false, and that I never made any such Confession, or gave Orders for printing the same. And I do further declare, that when I sent the Letter to Mr Samuel Betts, to bestow something upon me towards my Support, I thought that he had received the Reward for taking me, but as I find he did not appear against me at the Assizes, I am convinced he had no Right to the same, and that Mr Blower is in no Fault, that Mr Betts had no share of the said Reward. And I do also declare, that Mr Blower was very favourable in giving in his Evidence against me at the Assizes, and that Mr Blower, nor no other Person swore against me at the Assizes, but that I was convicted upon my own

Confession

Confession: And laftly, I do in Juftice to Mr Blower, publifh this as the real Truth, and in Vindication of his Character againft the many falfe Afperfions and Reflections he may be charged or chargeable with; and I humbly beg Pardon, and hope that Mr Blower will forgive me the many Injuries I have done him In Witnefs to the Truth of what is above written, I the faid Benjamin Barker, as a dying Man, and not long to live, have hereunto fet my Hand, this 7th Day of April, in the Year of our Lord 1750

        Sign'd BENJAMIN BARKER.

Attefted by
- John Lough
- Thomas Hinde
- Sam White S his Mark
- Matthew Joye,
- John Fauntleroy, of Chelmsford.

Church Wardens and Overfeers of the Poor of the Parifh of Chelmsford

Barker having been refpited fo long, was in great Hopes of being reprieved for Tranfportation, and when he was inform'd the Dead-Warrant was come down, he was in great Agonies, and faid he was forry he had ever fign'd the above Advertifement

He behaved very penitent while he was under Sentence of Death, and the Morning of his Execution after his Irons were knock'd off the Minifter came and preached a Sermon fuitable to the Occafion in the Goal, at which he likewife behaved very penitent, and afterwards received the Sacrament. He then was hand-cuff'd, and walk'd to the Gallows as is ufual.

At the Place of Execution,

He behaved very penitent, own'd the Fact, and the Justice of his Sentence, advised the Spectators to take Warning by him, and after spending some time in Prayer, called on God to have Mercy on him, was then turned off, and, after hanging the usual time, was cut down and buried near the Gallows.

F I N I S.